DISCOVER TO DELIVER

Agile Product Planning and Analysis

Ellen Gottesdiener and Mary Gorman

Published by EBG Consulting, Inc.
Printed in the United States of America

Library of Congress Control Number: 2012943771

ISBN 978-0-9857879-0-5
10 9 8 7 6 5 4 3 2 1
First printing, August 2012

The product partners continually

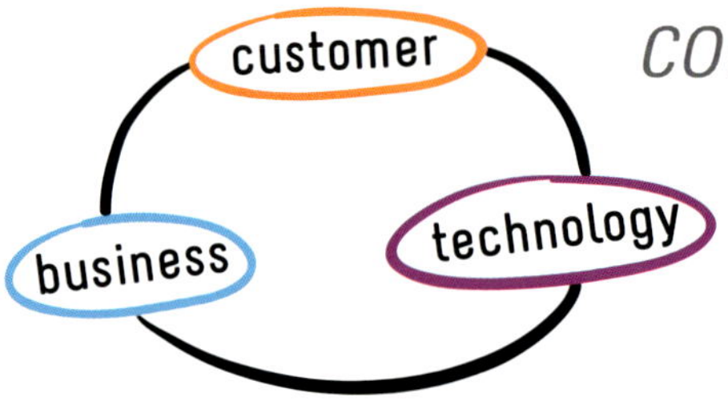

collaborate to

The partners

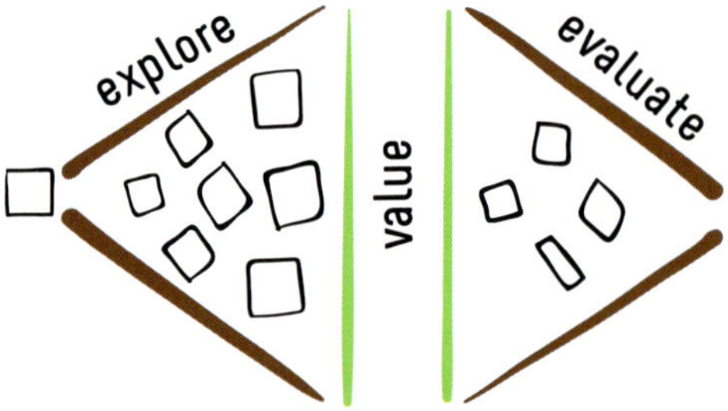

They identify and

cohesive chunks of high-value options and

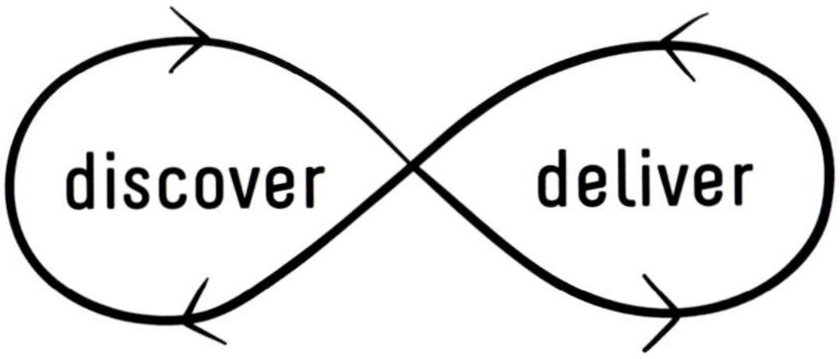

the evolving product.

options for the

7 Product Dimensions.

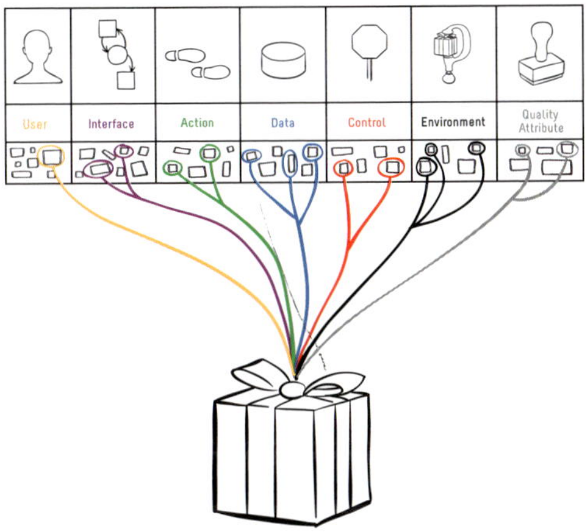

allocate them to plans

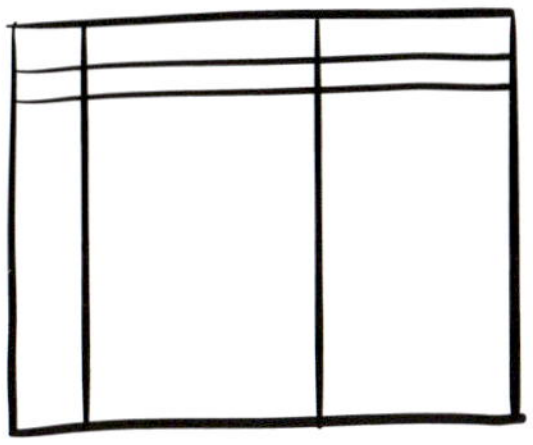

at all views.

CASE STUDY

Read how the Squeeky Kleen team plans and analyzes the company's product needs in three work sessions using the 7 Product Dimensions.

BIG CONCEPTS

Understand the product, partner, value, plan, and structured conversation concepts.

7 DIMENSIONS

Delve into the 7 Product Dimensions and their relationships.

CONVERSATION

Learn how to use the structured conversation to explore, evaluate, and confirm product needs at all levels of planning, as shown in the Squeeky Kleen case study.

ADAPT

Find ways to adapt these practices for your situation.

TOOLS & TECHNIQUES

See examples of a variety ways to engage in rich structured conversations about product needs, as shown in the Squeeky Kleen case study.

GLOSSARY

Look up the meaning of key words.

CONTENTS

PREFACE

You and your team need to deliver a product that's critical to your organization's success. Where do you start?

Or you're in the midst of planning, analyzing, and building the product, and you need help. What do you do next?

You're focused on the goal—delivering a valued product that delights your customer. You know your team needs support from multiple disciplines: business analysis, coaching, information architecture, product delivery and support, product management, project management, software development, testing and quality assurance, user experience, and more.

How can people from these diverse disciplines work together in a way that rapidly produces valued results?

This book describes essential practices that you can use in your daily work to rapidly discover product needs so that you can deliver valued results, and it gives you a visual language to streamline and simplify your planning and analysis. Our goal is to provide you and your team members with practical guidance in how to collaborate continually to discover and deliver an evolving product.

The Context

Discover to Deliver: Agile Product Planning and Analysis reflects our ongoing work with a variety of organizations to improve their product development. Many are using Agile and Lean practices. Others are using more traditional development approaches. They all need practices that work in diverse situations. This book is grounded in good practices synthesized from software and systems engineering, business analysis, product and project management, and group teamwork and collaboration.

We use "Agile" in our title. By *Agile*, we mean the family of practices for building software using iterative and incremental development. *Lean* practices focus on maximizing customer value while minimizing waste. For simplicity, we use "Agile" as an umbrella term that incorporates both Agile and Lean practices.

Note: We don't aim to provide a primer on Agile, Lean, or Kanban. We draw upon, but don't describe, the basics of good elicitation techniques, such as contextual inquiry, facilitated workshops, observation, prototyping, and user experience design. Nor do we describe the foundational practices of product or project management, product design and development, or even development of your business case. There are excellent books on these topics. You will find them on the book's website, www.DiscoverToDeliver.com.

Our Inspirations

In our work, we stand on the shoulders of many others who inspired and energized us. To the many authors of *Business Model Generation*—thank you! The design and elegance of this book and practices have been inspirational. We've also been influenced by a number of leaders in the Agile/Lean, product and project management, and business analysis communities. These people are leaders in continual learning. We want to call out those who in particular have influenced our work and provided inspiration, ideas, or encouragement. Our gratitude to Gojko Adzic, Scott Ambler, David Anderson, Kathleen Barret, Kevin Brennan, Greg Cohn, Mike Cohn, Lisa Crispin, Tom Gilb, Janet Gregory, Ron Jeffries, Henrick Kniberg, Jim Highsmith, Gladys Lam, Brian Lawley, Chris Matts, Dan North, Roman Pichler, Mary Poppendieck, Tom Poppendieck, Don Reinertsen, Eric Reis, Ron Ross, Jim Shore, Jean Tabaka, Dave Thomas, and Rob Thomsett.

Our Appreciations

We appreciate our friends, colleagues, reviewers, and loved ones for their support and patience throughout the journey of discovery and delivery of this book.

We gratefully acknowledge our reviewers for their feedback and suggestions. The following people gave us feedback for one or more of the book's internal releases. They played a key role in helping us verify and validate the book. Any errors that remain are ours alone. Thank you to Gojko Adzic, Joy Beatty, Jeff Bipes, Matt Block, Susan Block, Laura Brandenburg, Susan Burk, Jeff Cochran, Greg Cohn, Lisa Crispin, Rachel Davies, Andrew Galbus, Bob Galen, Tom Grant, Janet Gregory, Dan Lefebvre, Chris Matts, Kent McDonald, Devon McGeary, Kate McGoey, Dan Mezick, Debbie Nipper, Roman Pichler, Scott Selhorst, Kamal Singh, Helen Strickland, Amy Washburn, and Barry Young.

We want to amplify our thanks to Tom Poppendieck, who provided vital guidance throughout all the releases. Tom, your thoughtful comments, suggestions, affirmations, and critiques helped us create a better book with each successive release. Thank you.

We are grateful to Bruce Plourde for his project management of the self-publication process and his excellent design eye. Thanks to Cheryl Landes for her precise indexing work, suggestions, and deep experience with the art of indexing. We were fortunate indeed to have Freedom Rodriguez as our artist and page designer. Thank you, Freedom, for your wonderful work—and for your patience with the many iterations and challenging schedule.

Thanks to Jim Gorman, visual artist extraordinaire, who helped us create the original versions of the key images in the book. Jim's visual sensibility, practical suggestions, and immense patience provided the foundation for the visual language we share with you.

Our special thanks to Tamar Duke-Cohan, who reviewed the book for several of the releases. For our final release, we were fortunate to have Tamar as our technical copy editor. Tamar provided excellent edits and suggestions—concise, direct, and spot-on—all under a tight deadline. We were fortunate to have her on our team.

We are appreciative of Betsy Hardinger, our magical fairy lady, whose copy edit wand waved over and over our book since its inception. Betsy was more than a copy editor to us. She prodded, encouraged, and mentored us through a wild and wondrous journey of discovery and delivery with wit and warmth.

We are deeply grateful to the people in many organizations whom we have worked with over many years. Your trust and partnership with us has made this book possible.

Our deepest appreciation goes to our spouses, our personal power. To Jeffrey and Jim, who endured this journey with patience, protein, and potions: thank you.

The Ongoing Conversation...

We hope you'll visit us at www.DiscoverToDeliver.com. You'll find updates, job aids, and more conversations about these essential practices, as well as ways to boost your productivity, tips on teamwork, and more.

We look forward to hearing from you!

Section 1

THE CASE STUDY

Let's get started

In Section 1, we jump into our case study. The idea is for you to see Discover to Deliver™ in action.

Concepts and practices begin in Section 2.

You'll note the use of *italics* the first time a glossary term is used.

THE CASE STUDY: Squeeky Kleen

To illustrate the practices in this book, we've created a fictitious company called Squeeky Kleen (abbreviated SK). Squeeky Kleen currently provides window cleaning services for residential properties. Eventually the company expects to expand. Management wants to add services such as window repairs, enter the commercial properties market, and franchise the business to multiple locations throughout North America and the world. SK is looking to automate many of its support and sales functions.

The SK management team has developed a *business model* to position the company for the expansion. The initial focus is to streamline the process of estimating and scheduling cleaning services for customers. The management team sees the cost of these improvements as a prudent investment and has chosen Apps-R-Us (a consulting firm) as their partner to deliver the appropriate tools.

The *product partners* decide to begin the development effort by focusing on the *Pre-View*, move to the *Now-View*, and then the *Big-View*. (This practice mirrors how many *Agile* teams get started. They start with the Pre-View to gain context, and then they dive into the Now-View. They save the long-term Big-View for later, after they have gained some experience and obtained feedback on delivered solutions.)

This flow—Pre-View, Now-View, Big-View—gets the Squeeky Kleen *delivery team* into the habit of regularly delivering a valued product. It also gives them time to learn and adapt their collaboration process and technical work.

The First Pre-View Planning and Analysis Session

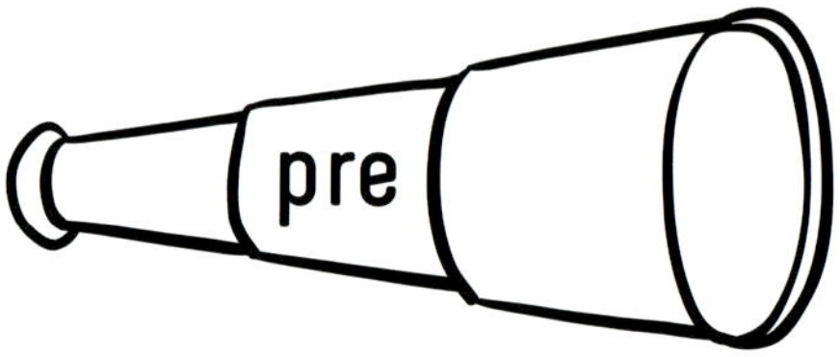

The Partners

The *product team* hails from the business, customer, and technology community. The people who are present at the first Pre-View *workshop* are noted with a star (*).

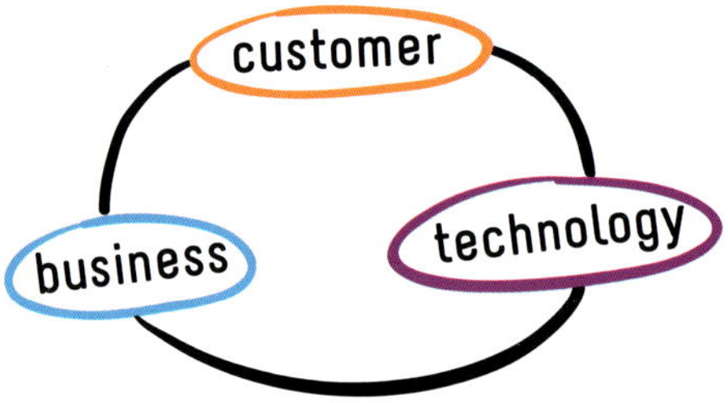

SK *Business Partners*

- Sal, Squeeky Kleen CEO, *Sponsor*
- Pat, SK Office Manager, *Product Champion**
- Sarah, Sales Manager

SK *Customer Partners*

- Squeeky Kleen customers and office staff, *users*

Apps-R-Us *Technology Partners*

- Lee, Information Architecture and Development*
- Ben, Planning and Analysis*
- Deb, Development*
- Ted, *User Experience* and Testing*

The Setting

The *partners* are meeting in a small room that has lots of contiguous wall space. The table is stocked with markers and stickies in different sizes and colors. Hanging on the walls (from prior preparatory work) are the following:

- A list of the partners' *value considerations*
- The *7 Product Dimensions Options board*

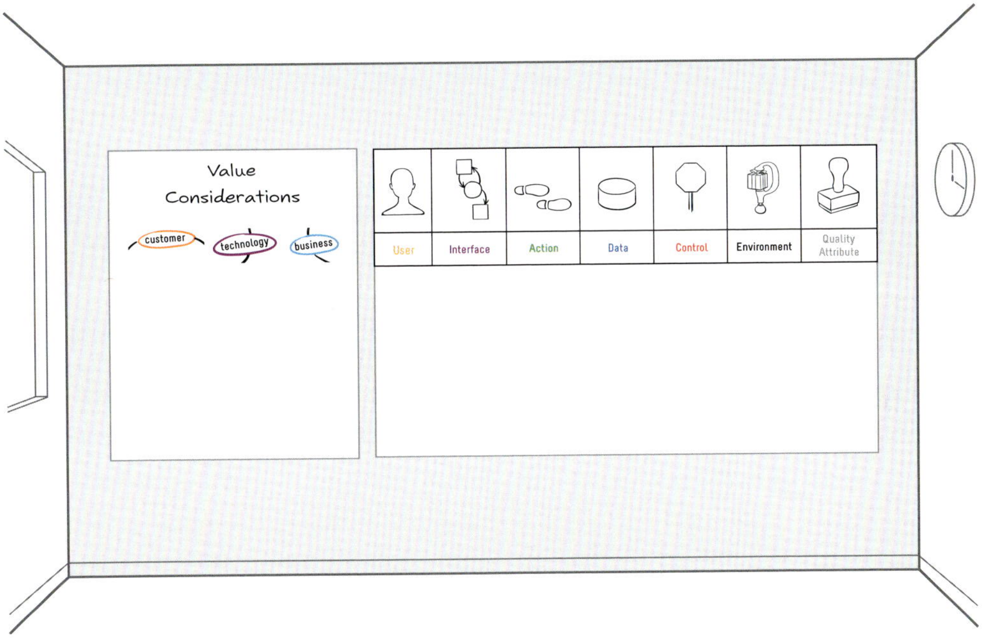

The 7 Product Dimensions Options Board

The Structured Conversation

We join the team as they conduct their Pre-View planning and analysis workshop using the *structured conversation*. As people arrive, Pat asks them to take a few minutes to review the materials on the walls before sitting down. She is the first to speak.

Pat: Okay, folks, thanks for coming.

Ben: Everybody settled in? Good. What we're doing today is defining what we'll actually release in the next four weeks. We'll be building and testing *increments* of the product every couple of weeks. This first *release* will lay the foundation to make SK's core business—providing window cleaning services—more efficient and is a vital step toward SK's longer-term *vision*. For today, let's get started on the Pre-View. In our next workshop we'll plan the first increment—the Now-View.

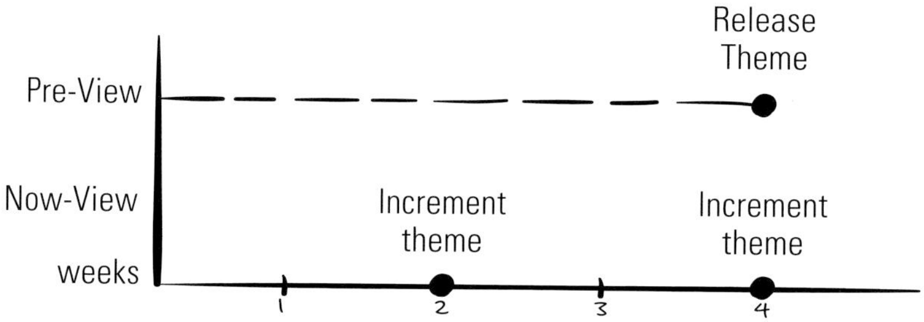

Pat: Last week Ben and I looked at several problems our SK people have calculating estimates for our services and communicating the estimates to customers. We've put them under the heading "Problems with Estimating." (She points to the "Problems with Estimating" poster.)

Problems with Estimating

- CSRs unintentionally use out-of-date prices.
- It's hard to quickly train new CSRs about our menu of services.
- Lack of coordinated "official" tools (some CSRs use calculators, some have created their own spreadsheets to do estimates).
- We don't save all estimates.
- Getting stuck on a call with a customer who doesn't know what services they need.

Deb: Remind me—what does CSR stand for?

Pat: Oh, sorry. "Customer service representative."

Any other questions? Okay. As you can see, there are lots of opportunities for improvement! So one approach we're considering is to give our customers direct access to an application that will calculate their estimates. Our *hypothesis* is that they'll like it, and from our operations perspective we'll save time and some money. I'll keep you posted on our progress. Please check out what we're showing as value considerations for the customers, specific to estimating. (She points to the poster.)

Customer Value Considerations

- Customers need to know the price for their specific cleaning needs. They want to get an accurate estimate, quickly.
- Customers want convenient access to SK estimates.

Ben dug a little deeper and outlined a customer *persona*. This persona stands for the customer we want to target with this product. (She points to the persona on the *User Dimension* of the Options board.)

Roger, The Customer

"Roger" values being a savvy shopper. He likes to compare prices and may want to speak with one of our satisfied customers to get a firsthand account of our services. He wants only environmentally safe products used on his property. When he first contacts SK, he may need some help identifying the types of surfaces he wants cleaned, and he doesn't want to waste time or feel ignorant if he doesn't know the specific names (such as transom window). Bottom line, Roger is cost and quality conscious, and in a bit of a hurry.

Pat: Okay, now let's look at the business and technology value considerations.

Business Value Considerations

CSRs needs

- Efficient workflow
- Support with mundane tasks, access to up-to-date data

Office Manager needs

- Improve CSR retention
- Reduce training time for new CSRs, reduce customers' current estimating complaints about actual cost vs. estimated price

Sales Manager needs

- Estimates to be done consistently using current pricing
- The customer to be informed about specific conditions that might influence their decision about using SK's services.

Technology Value Considerations

- Support a variety of ways for SK staffers to interface with the application, e.g., online, mobile.

After some discussion, Pat guides the group back to focusing on what can be accomplished in the next four weeks for their first release.

Pat: We started looking into the estimating problems a few months ago (she points to the poster again). We're collecting metrics on the time it takes to estimate services, as well as accuracy. We've been analyzing the metrics to find out what and where we can improve. You're welcome to review the metrics—I'll email them out later.

Lee: Yes, and I'd like to add a value consideration—making sure the technology platform we use going forward is *scalable* and *modifiable*. (Pat adds that item under the Technology Value Considerations on the poster.)

Pat: We want to use this first release to learn how to use new technologies. Ultimately our goal is to save money and time to build, test, and deliver a high-value product. (She writes "Easy Estimator" on a big sticky and puts it on the 7 Product Dimensions Options board, a.k.a. Options board.) Ben asked me to come up with a *theme* for our release. So here it is! Easy

Estimator. Our purpose today is to explore and evaluate the scope of this release. Ted's been observing the CSRs, using what he calls *contextual inquiry*. Ted?

Ted: I've been watching the folks in action. Lots of challenges. Most customers call to request an estimate, but some requests come in through the office fax, and even a few e-mails. CSRs have pieces of information stuck everywhere—you know, stickies on their computers, that sort of thing. Or they have to fumble through binders to look up types of windows—there are lots of different kinds, and each one has its own price. As Ben mentioned, some of the CSRs use calculators, and some have homemade spreadsheets. I'm not kidding. It's a mess.

Ben: Okay, we're talking about who could use the Easy Estimator application—that goes in the User column. (He points to the Options board and writes under the User section, "CSR Estimator.")

Ted: I also went with some senior cleaners to do on-site estimates. That was really informative! They have their own set of issues to deal with. Right now they're stuck with an old paper form they use to enter the site details, including any special equipment that might be needed, such as ladders or even scaffolding. They typically walk around the property, then go back to the truck to finish up the estimate. Sometimes they have to look up pricing for less common windows. When the estimate is completed, they drop it off in the office. A senior CSR double-checks the calculations and mails a copy to the customer. There are lots of areas for improvement!

Ben: Right—the On-site Estimators are another kind of user. (He adds "On-Site Estimator" in the User area of the Options board.)

Deb: Why do we do some estimates on-site?

Pat: We send the On-site Estimators out on big or complicated jobs. Or some customers just want a guaranteed price. Without an on-site estimate, it's not guaranteed.

Lee: So we'd be looking at giving the on-site estimators a tablet, with a mobile app? We'd need to consider the conditions it's used under—nasty weather, thrown into the truck, printing. Things like that. (Ben adds "mobile device" to the *Environment* section of the Options board.)

Ted: What about having the customer get an estimate directly, without having to go through a CSR? Can we do that?

Pat: I sure hope so, down the road. But we don't know if it's worth the investment. Will customers really use it? That's the question. Our hypothesis is that they'll like it, and from our operations perspective we'll save time and some money.

Lee: Let's explore that for a moment. I was thinking it would support our overall goal if our customers could communicate with SK 24/7, at their convenience. I'm not talking about having CSRs working those hours. I'm looking at the customer value "convenience" —not having to wait to get an estimate during normal business hours. (Ben adds "Customer Self-Service Estimator" in the User area of the Options board.)

Pat: So that would be another category of user. But before we jump in with both feet, we need to confirm that our customers really would use this. Let's call this the "Customer Self-Service Estimating" hypothesis. How can we test this?

Lee: Well, we could build a web page to count how many people indicate their interest in the *feature*. Is that what you have in mind?

Ted: That's really simple, and it could provide some useful data. We need some way to measure customer interest in that. Yes, I could prototype a few interfaces for the screen.

Lee: So the customer comes to the web site looking to get their windows cleaned. What if we let them fill out a form to get an estimate? Any time, 24/7. Or we could have them enter their details—name, address, desired date. We queue up the request—

Pat: Yes, I love that idea.

Deb raises a yellow card. (This yellow index card visually signals to the group to ask, "Do we want to continue discussing this now?" Per their agreement, anyone can hold up a yellow card.)

Pat: Thanks, Deb. We are getting off-track. Let me just close up the hypothesis topic. I need to do some research on what we'd actually be testing for this. As you like to call it, Ben, *validated learning*. There is a risk here that we might build it and our customers won't use it, so I want to be sure we're making a decent investment decision. Ted, after this session, can you help me figure out some metrics? (Ted nods.)

Ben: Okay. We've got three user *options* for the Estimator role. (He points to the Options board showing the CSR, On-Site, and Customer Self-Service estimators.) We need to establish the value of each option. What are the benefits and risks we need to consider in order to make a decision? (He sketches a *user role map* and posts it on the Options board.)

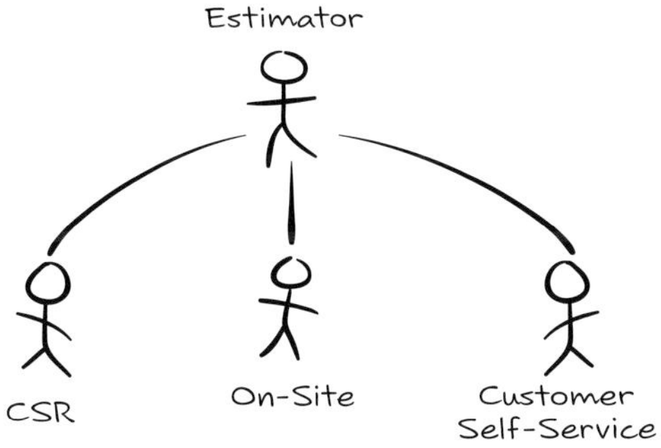

The team has already agreed to use the Value Considerations list to evaluate the options. In discussing the three User options they've identified, they immediately note that the Customer Self-Service Estimator will be addressed in the hypothesis Pat has asked Lee to work on, so it is out of scope for the first release.

Next, they evaluate the *benefits* and *risks* of addressing the needs of On-Site Estimators. The *operational environment* (such as weather conditions) will require investigating and testing new mobile technologies. Currently only a few workers are authorized to do on-site estimates, Pat says, and they're highly experienced.

Next, Pat points out the benefits and risks of focusing on the CSR Estimator role. There are trainee, junior, and senior CSRs. The majority of the estimates are produced by the junior CSRs. Because SK is experiencing high turnover of junior CSRs, the team's collective decision is to focus on the Junior CSR Estimator for the first release of Easy Estimator.

Pat takes a marker and puts a big star next to "CSR Estimator" on the Options board.

Ben adds the CSR life cycle *states* "trainee," "junior," and "senior" to the User column on the Options board. He stars the junior state.

> Pat: So we've agreed; our focus is on the Junior CSR Estimator. Let's talk about how we will confirm that we've built the right thing—the business outcomes we expect to get.

They come up with the following criteria and hang them near the Value Considerations poster:

Customer value: "Quick"

- Reduce the elapsed time to provide the estimated price for an average customer request from 7 minutes to 3 minutes or less.
- CSRs will pick up a customer phone call within 3 rings or less (now it's 5).
- CSRs will capture the estimate details so that the same customer can call later to schedule another job without having to re-specify them.

Business (Sales) value: "Accurate" estimates

- Reduce the customers' current estimating complaints about actual cost vs. estimates by at least half.
- Estimates will be based on current prices.

Pat asks for help in transforming these into SMART (Specific, Measurable, Attainable, Realistic, Time-based) *objectives*. Ben offers to consult with her after the meeting. The team discusses the who, how, and when of conducting their *validation* to confirm the value of the release.

> Ted: I've noticed that sometimes the CSRs use an old price sheet, or when they are under pressure, they use the wrong price to calculate the estimate—especially the trainee and junior CSRs. Or I've seen customers call back and ask for an estimate again and get a different price. That's a deal-killer.

Pat: You're right—these are big risks. Estimating—and scheduling, for that matter—are dependent on having the service details. That's an important *dependency*. Sarah in Sales has been asking for months if she can have a way to easily share updates of the service details with the SK staff. (Ted sketches a simple *context diagram* on the Options board showing the inputs and outputs.)

Ben: Okay, I think we're ready to explore the actions, data, and controls for Easy Estimator (He points to those areas on the Options board and distributes a handout.) Here's a draft list of the *events* involved with estimating prices. Can we split into two teams to review and revise, as well as add the planned *responses?*

The two teams get busy and post their results on the Options board's Action area. Then the entire team reviews them.

Event: A customer asks a general question about SK services.
Response: Provide answer to question.
Scenarios: • Frequently Asked Questions (FAQs) • Referrals • Payment methods • List of SK service areas • List of SK services descriptions, and prices (including discounts) • Insurance and bonding policies

Event: A customer requests a cleaning estimate.
Response: Provide estimated price amount.
Scenarios: • The CSR Estimator enters the estimate details, shares calculated estimated price • The CSR Estimator determines that the customer's requested services cannot be estimated without an on-site survey • The CSR Estimator runs into difficulty completing the estimate and asks another CSR for help

Event: A customer provides a picture of a unique window and requests an estimate to clean it.
Response: Offer to set up an on-site visit to provide an estimate.

Event: A customer is ready to schedule estimated services
Response: Search for the estimate. Schedule the job.
Scenarios: • The CSR Scheduler finds the estimate and schedules the job • The CSR Scheduler cannot find the estimate • The customer changes some of the details

Event: The Sales Manager changes the service details
Response: Capture details. Communicate service details to SK staff.
Scenarios: • Change service description • Update price • Add image of window type, e.g., picture of window

The team discusses the benefits and risks involved with each event. Deb questions the event "A customer is ready to schedule estimated services." Pat shares that currently only on-site estimates are saved, and then only for 90 days. But for the future, it would be very helpful to save all estimates. It would definitely speed up scheduling, which aligns with the customer value "quick."

They decide that, for this release, the highest value is to focus on the simple request for an estimate. Pat goes to the Options board and stars the event "A customer requests a cleaning estimate."

Ben: Let me make sure I understand. We aren't going to come up with any new ways to help respond to customers' FAQs?
Pat: No, we'll just have to get by for now.
Ted: What about the one for the Sales Manager changing service details?

They consider building a application that would let Sales enter and store the updated service data, including the start and expiration dates of prices, which are needed for audit purposes. A repository of service data could become the source of record for all current and future SK applications, including Easy Estimator.

Pat: This is a great idea.

She adds Service in the data area of the Options board, and puts a star next to it. Ben adds the Sales Manager as a user on the Options board.

Ted: Getting back to the event, "A customer requests a cleaning estimate." In essence, we're going to get started by creating an application for the CSRs to use. They will be able to input the customer's requested cleaning services and see the estimated price. Right?

Pat: That's right. This seems very simplistic, but it has high value for us as a business. There is no way we can roll out different types of services, like repairs, or expand our markets if we can't give our customers fast, reliable estimates for our basic services. And it will absolutely be needed for franchising.

Ted: Sounds good.

Lee: Can we talk about the data now?

Ben: Based on our conversation so far, I'm going to add more data options to the Options board. (He writes: Customer, FAQ, Estimate, Window Type, Payment Method, Property.)

Lee: What type of properties are you serving? Both residential and commercial?

Pat: Commercial properties are in the growth plan, but first we need to get our residential estimating and scheduling activities fine-tuned.

Ben: Hold on. Are we using "property type" and "property" interchangeably? This could lead to confusion. We all need to be "*glossary guardians*" so we don't waste time going over these terms again and again.

Pat: You're right that it can be confusing! We define a "property" as a physical place where a service takes place, both the structure itself as well as its physical location. And be aware that sometimes we call it the "service location."

Ted: I heard the term "property" being used during my observations at the office. (He glances at Pat, who nods in agreement.)

Ben: Then let's use "property" as we move forward.

Everyone nods. Lee adds the term and definition to the *Glossary* poster. Pat then mentions that there are "non-standard" property types, such as historic residences. They typically have unique characteristics that don't easily fit the common window types, and in the past it's been risky to service them. For that reason, SK's policy is to always conduct on-site estimates for these properties.

Since the team excluded on-site estimating from the first release of Easy Estimator, by default they agree that only "standard" residential property types are in scope. Ben adds "non-standard" to the glossary and jots it down in the *Data Dimension* area on the Options board.

Next, Ben starts sketching a *data model*. In the meantime the team uses the opportunity to add glossary definitions for "window type" and "customer." The team continues exploring data as Ted hands out some sample estimates that he drafted while observing the CSRs last week.

> Deb: These examples are really helpful. In addition to window cleaning, I saw ones for cleaning solar panels, exterior light fixtures, mirrors, and sliding glass doors. Are they all included in this release?
>
> Pat: Well, there are even more things we clean—bay windows, gutters, and even chandeliers! But the vast majority of our business is in window cleaning. Another factor is that most of the non-window types of cleaning—like solar panels—require on-site estimates. So for Easy Estimator we'll focus on window cleaning services only.

They continue the discussion about the window types. Because the cleaning price depends on the type of window, the CSR and the customer need the same understanding of these terms. Pat explains that customers often don't know the terminology for different types of windows, and they need explanations. Lee recalls the event the team just looked at: "A customer provides a picture of a unique window and requests an estimate to clean it." They agree that it would give SK a significant competitive advantage if a customer could send in pictures of a window and have the CSR look up the specific price and calculate an estimate.

But Pat holds firm. She needs a simple solution now. The photo option will have to wait. They agree that there are other, short-term ways to help with this issue, such as providing standard descriptions for CSRs to use when discussing window types. Ted offers to look into it after the session.

Ben: You know, as we talk it's crucial that we understand the data needs, certainly when we're designing and building the *interfaces*, and for testing.

Lee: This is a good time to stop and identify the high-value data—the data that's needed to support the high-value actions. (Pat adds stars next to the following data options: Estimate, Cleaning and Window Type, and Property, Residential, Standard.)

Ben and Lee draft an *interaction matrix* to cross-check the actions with the data. The matrix compactly outlines the actions that create, read, update, and delete the data. They all clearly see the dependency estimating has on the window type data.

Ben: (Points to the *Control Dimension* on the Options board.) We need to get an idea of the *business policies* related to the high-value options we've identified so far—how many there are and how complicated. They will make a difference when we gauge the size of *stories*.

They discuss numerous policies specific to on-site estimates until Deb holds up the yellow card, reminding them that on-site estimates are out of scope. The team then turns its focus to the in-scope event.

Pat: Oh, by the way, have I mentioned there's another opportunity we need to address? (The team smiles.) Some customers have complained that they weren't told our estimate policies—most importantly, that we don't guarantee the price unless we conduct an on-site survey of the property, as someone mentioned earlier. (She adds the policy "off-site estimate is an approximate price" to the Options board.)

Ted: I'll check into what we can do to help with that. Pat: For this release, it's essential that customers be informed about SK's policy—an off-site estimate is an approximate price. (She adds the policy on the Options board.)

The team reviews the Options board.

Ben: Okay, the next step is to assemble the starred options into cohesive stories.

Pre-View: Easy Estimator

High-value options are noted with a star (*)

	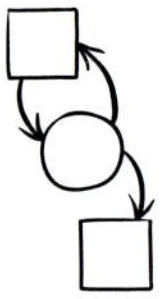	
User	**Interface**	**Action**
Estimator Roles* CSR* Customer Self-Service On-Site	Customer to CSR Estimator* phone* fax email	Event: Customer asks general question about SK services Response: Provide answer Event: Customer requests a cleaning estimate* Response: Provide estimated price amount*
CSR States* Senior Junior* Trainee	On-site Estimator to the application mobile device CSR to application* UI*	Event: Customer provides picture of unique window and requests an estimate to clean it Response: Offer to set up on-site visit to provide estimate Event: Customer is ready to schedule estimated services Response: Search for estimate, Schedule job
Sales Manager*	Sales Manager to the application manual UI	Event: Sales Manager changes service details* Response: Capture service detail, Communicate service detail to staff*

Note: This area of the Options board is used for models.

Options Board

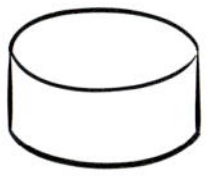	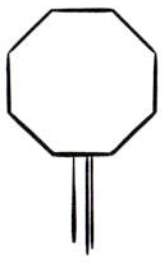		
Data	Control	Environment	Quality Attribute
Customer FAQ Estimate* Service Type* cleaning* window* other repair Property type* commercial residential* non-standard standard* Property Payment Method	Non-standard property services must be estimated on-site* Off-site estimate is an approximate price*	Off-site SK Office*	Usability* Availability* Scalability Installability Performance*

Due to space limitations the models are not shown.
See www.DiscoverToDeliver.com for samples.

The team defines a few stories. They estimate the work effort to deliver the stories using "t-shirt sizes" (small, medium, large, extra large).

As a CSR Estimator,
I need to provide an off-site cleaning estimate
for a standard residential property's windows,
so the customer can decide whether to use
SK's services.

Work effort estimate: medium

The team writes the *scenario:*

Roger Smith has moved into a new house. He calls Squeeky Kleen to get an estimate for cleaning. The CSR asks Roger what type of windows he wants cleaned, and how many of each type. The CSR provides an estimated price for the requested services, as well as some key differentiators of SK's capabilities. Roger will use the estimate to determine whether to select SK to provide the cleaning services.

The team notes the related high-value options to the story:

User state: Junior CSR Estimator
Interface: CSR to customer - phone
CSR to Easy Estimator - basic UI
Controls: An off-site estimate is an approximate price.
Non-standard property services must be estimated on-site.
Operational Environment: SK Office
Development Environment: TBD
Quality Attributes: Availability, Performance and Usability specifics TBD

The team writes the scenario:

> The SK management team has decided to update window type details. Sarah needs to let the SK staff know about the changes and when to start using them for estimating and scheduling.

As the SK Sales Manager,
I need to communicate cleaning service details
so estimating and scheduling can be as efficient
as possible.

Work effort estimate: small

Deb sketches a context diagram that represents the stories.

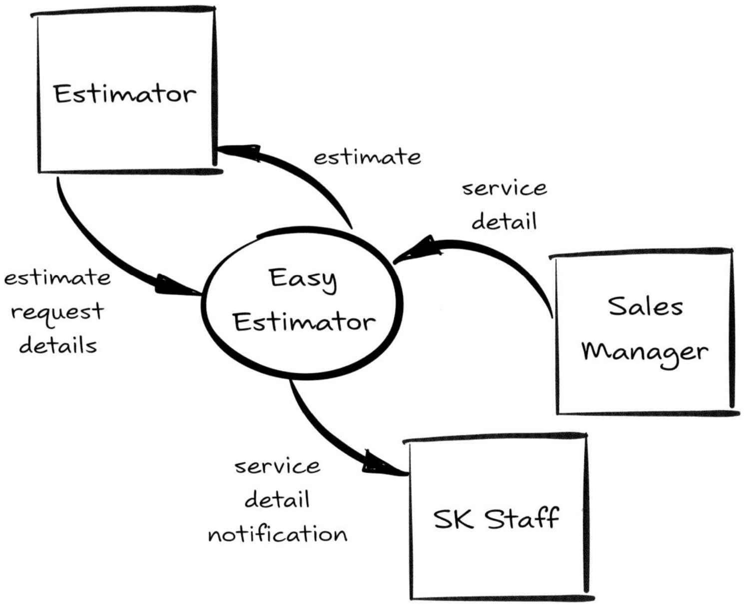

The Structured Conversation Wrap Up

Ben asks the team to help him check whether they've covered all the bases. Following is a summary of their brief discussion:

- They observed and analyzed the business processes that need to be improved.
- Their decisions have been grounded in the value considerations of all partners, balancing benefits, risks, dependencies, and the estimates to develop the product.
- They addressed each of the 7 Product Dimensions throughout the conversation (and used models when helpful).
- They actively worked on the glossary.

The team agrees to meet in two days to explore and evaluate stories to be completed in the next two weeks (Now-View).

In the meantime, they agree to the following:

- Pat and Ben will review the Options board, create a small *backlog* (or *queue*) of work in the form of stories, and array them on a *story map* to review with the team later.
- Ted will create some sketches for the Easy Estimator interfaces, referencing the stories, the Options board, and notes from his contextual inquiry work.
- Ben will draft a CSR persona.
- Lee will begin researching operational environment options by inventorying the current office equipment devices, browsers, processors, and network servers.
- Ted will begin research into a typical customer profile for the candidate solution to test the self-service hypothesis. He will interview customers, draft a persona, and sketch out possible interface screens.

Pat: Anything else? Okay, everybody—great work. To come full circle, I'll schedule an review for a month after the launch of this first release of Easy Estimator. At that time we'll determine whether the objectives are being met. We need to learn what's working and consider next steps. I want to be sure we're getting the value we anticipate for Easy Estimator. At the end of this *delivery cycle*, I'd like us to demonstrate to Sal that we can provide immediate relief for pressing issues and offer process improvements while we're aiming for the bigger vision.

The team then devotes 20 minutes to holding a *retrospective* of their first planning session. Ben facilitates.

Together, they review their group process and reflect on what worked and what might be improved. They note the key retrospective learning points on a poster:

- Everyone was well prepared and actively engaged.
- The Options board was very useful.
- It is helpful to use quick and simple analysis models to visualize product needs.
- We used the "yellow card" playfully but powerfully to stay on track.
- It was useful to apply the value considerations lists throughout the session.

The team members spend a few minutes agreeing on specific improvement actions. They add these to the Learning Points poster:

- Use dark-colored markers when writing on the Options board so everyone can easily read the text.
- Ben will brief Ray, the senior CSR, who will participate in the Now-View planning session, on the planning session process.
- Prepare for the next planning session by rereading the persona for the CSR.

The First Now-View Planning and Analysis Session

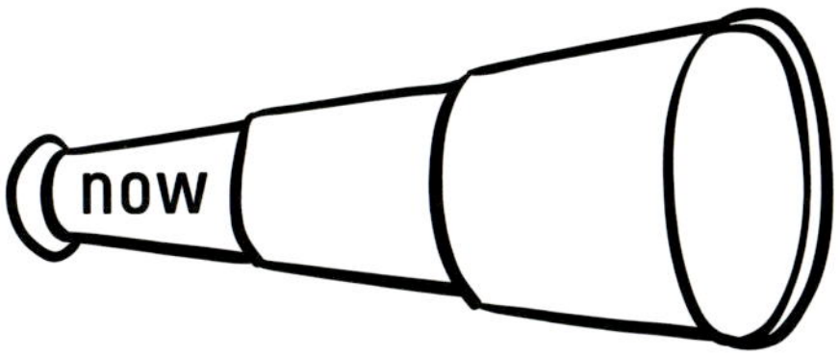

The Partners

The people who are present at the first Now-View meeting are noted with a star (*).

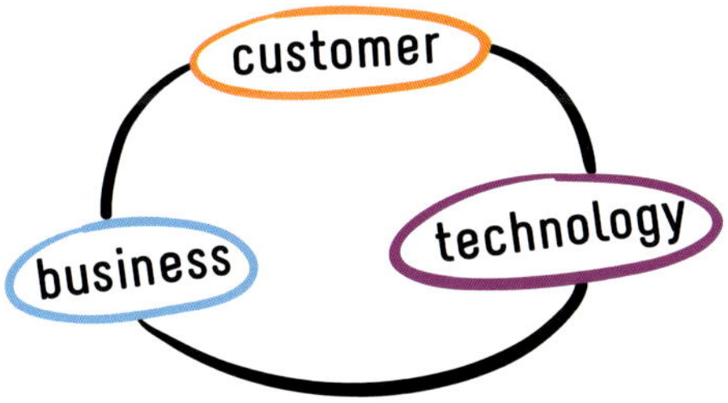

SK Business Partners
- Sal, Squeeky Kleen CEO, Sponsor
- Pat, SK Office Manager, Product Champion*
- Sarah, Sales Manager

SK Customer Partners
- Squeeky Kleen customers and office staff, users
- Ray, SK senior CSR*

Apps-R-Us Technology Partners
- Lee, Architecture and Development*
- Ben, Planning and Analysis*
- Deb, Development*
- Ted, User Experience and Testing*

The Setting

Back in the team room.

We join the team as they conduct their Now-View planning and analysis workshop using the structured conversation. In their Pre-View workshop a few days ago, the partners focused on the first release, which they dubbed "Easy Estimator." Today they're exploring and evaluating what to deliver in the first *iteration*. The *candidate solutions* they discuss today will be the basis for the work they will do during the next two weeks.

The Structured Conversation

As everyone settles in, Pat introduces Ray, SK's most experienced Customer Service Representative (CSR). Ted has been working with Ray during the past week to learn about the CSRs' daily activities. CSRs will be the main users of the product the team is building in this first release.

Pat shares the objectives for this release, which she researched and documented after the team's Pre-View workshop. She reminds the team that the objectives are based on the *value decisions* they discussed, that she did her best to make them SMART, and that she reviewed them with Sal (Squeeky Kleen's CEO) and Ray just before this session. She hangs up a poster with the following objectives and walks through it with the team:

One month after the launch of Easy Estimator:

> 90% of the estimates provided by the Easy Estimator application will be completed in less than 3 minutes ("Completed" is defined as "total estimated price is displayed on the screen").
>
> 95% of the CSRs will use the Easy Estimator application for relevant estimating.
>
> Customer satisfaction rating will be 80% or higher, based on a survey of customers who received estimates calculated by Easy Estimator.
>
> The Sales Manager will be able to directly update a service price and description in Easy Estimator in less than 1 minute.

Pat: It's important to remember that these are conjectures, and we will need to confirm them against *actual results*. A month after the launch of Easy Estimator, we'll assess its impact. SK wants to make good decisions about candidate solutions, and we'll take a continual learning approach in short delivery cycles.

Next, Pat holds up a large sticky with her suggested theme for the Now-View: "Out of the Blocks." She places it at the top of the 7 Product Dimensions Options board.

Ted: I like that. It shows how we're getting set to move quickly. (Everyone nods.)

Pat reminds the team that the primary hands-on users for Easy Estimator are the CSRs. The team takes a few minutes to review the CSR persona Ben created ("Charlie"), which is also posted in the User area of the Options board.

Persona Name: Charlie, a junior Customer Service Rep (CSR)

Description 	In constant communication with customers and contractors. Must satisfy customers' needs in timely, courteous way. Includes all activities surrounding customer jobs: estimating, scheduling, canceling, rescheduling, etc. Acts as liaison with Accounting. "A good day is when I can respond to 90% of new customer requests within 3 minutes." Part-time employee of SK, paid by the hour, receives bonuses when exceeds service level agreements. Knowledgeable about business, maintains good relationship with cleaners. Amiable, problem solver, proficient with standard office software products.
Needs	Easy access to essential, up-to-date customer and property data. Rapid way to communicate with cleaners. Relief from mundane tasks, e.g., reminding customer of upcoming job.
Goals	Provide efficient and personal service. Exceed SK's service level agreements to earn bonus.

(Throughout the session, the team continually works on the Options board by adding and valuing options and drawing *analysis models*.)

Pat: Okay, folks, based on our decision out of the Pre-View planning, we're going to focus on helping the CSRs calculate cleaning estimates—even if it starts out as a very simple application. The plan is to eventually have a version on our web site that customers can use—the hypothesis we've been calling "Customer Self-Service Estimating." So we've agreed to start exploring that hypothesis—or as you sometimes call it, candidate solution—to see if it will appeal to customers. We're working on metrics to confirm whether we will invest in offering it. For now, let's focus on what it will take to deliver "Out of the Blocks." (She points to the story from the Pre-View session.)

As a CSR Estimator,
I need to provide an off-site cleaning estimate
for a standard residential property's windows,
so the customer can decide whether to use SK's
services.

Work effort estimate: medium

Pat continues: Let's jump right in. Remember Roger, our customer persona? (She points to the User area of the Options board.) To win Roger's business, we need to help our CSRs, especially the new hires. We understand they need quick, accurate job aids to help them converse with the Rogers out there. It's vital for our reputation that the CSRs provide consistent, accurate estimates to customers. Any questions about that? Okay, so it's also important that the CSRs inform Roger about our differentiators—what makes us different, and better, than the competition. The two big differentiators that especially appeal to our customers are that we use environmentally safe cleaning products and do full-service window cleaning—at no additional cost. By "full service," we mean, when our cleaners clean the window they actually open the window and clean the sill and tracks too. Believe it or not, that's not common practice in our industry. Many of our competitors don't do that, or they charge extra for it.

Ben: Understood. I think it would help if we take a look at some scenarios for this story that Ray and I wrote yesterday. Ray, can you walk us through those?

Ray reviews the scenarios, which are written on index cards. Deb puts them on the Options board in the Actions area. As they study the scenarios that they need to deliver, they begin to discuss the estimated price that CSRs provide to the customer.

Pat: Our legal adviser repeatedly cautions us to be very clear that any estimated price determined off-site is an approximate price. It is essential that the CSRs explain that, for an accurate price, we must have an SK person conduct an on-site survey of the customer's property, and we'll be happy to set up an appointment for that at no charge. We need the CSRs to clearly and consistently communicate this.

Lee: I remember hearing something about a minimum price. What about that?

Ray: Yes, that's really important. We have a minimum charge for doing any cleaning. Right now it's $60, but management changes it every year or so. So if a customer just wants two windows cleaned, they're still charged the minimum.

The team discusses these rules for a few minutes, and Ben volunteers to write down a few scenarios during a break.

Pat: I forgot to mention that we offer certain customers discounts, and sometimes we offer coupons. They need to be factored into the estimates.

Ben: Okay, we'll need Data and Control options for "discount price" and "coupon."

Lee: Well, those will add complexity! Are you sure this release can still be called "Easy Estimating"?

Pat quickly decides that she can wait for a future release to incorporate discounts of all kinds.

Pat: The other thing I want to be sure we cover is this: when the CSRs provide an estimate, they need to remember to emphasize how we exceed our competitors' services—those full services I mentioned a minute ago. This is what often convinces a customer to use us. And I'm not sure all CSRs are consistent about how they communicate these points.

Ray: You're right! Some of the CSRs forget or stumble on that.

Ben: Pat, can you give us the standard language that should be used?

Pat: I'll ask the Sales folks to help.

Deb: We could add the wording on the estimating screen so the CSRs can easily reference them.

Ted: That might require some work. Remember, the driving point of the UI is enabling the CSR to very quickly input the necessary data. So, for each window type they enter the number that need to be cleaned. Then the application calculates and displays the estimated price, and a total price. If we add what we're calling the standard language, it may make the screen pretty busy. Pat, once we get the final standard language text, I'll draft a few mockups so we can figure out how and where to add it to the screen.

Ray: I want to point out that the junior CSRs sometimes waste our customer's time by not asking them the right questions in the right order. (He looks at Ted and Ben.) You saw some of that when you observed in the office, right?

Ted: Yes, for sure. We want to guide the CSR to ask questions in a sequence that helps the customer quickly determine if Squeeky Kleen can even provide the services they want. We don't want CSRs wasting their time—or the customer's time.

Ray shares a diagram he drew while talking with Ted yesterday. The *business process diagram* shows the flow of the typical estimating actions—and his hopes for what the new application will be able to do.

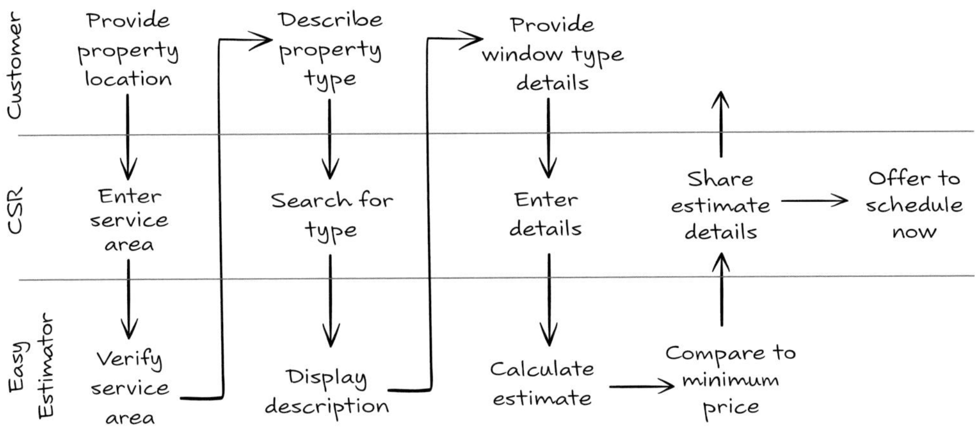

Ted: While Ray was doing the process diagram, I sketched my first cut of a *prototype* for the estimating screen. Please—remember it's only a rough draft.

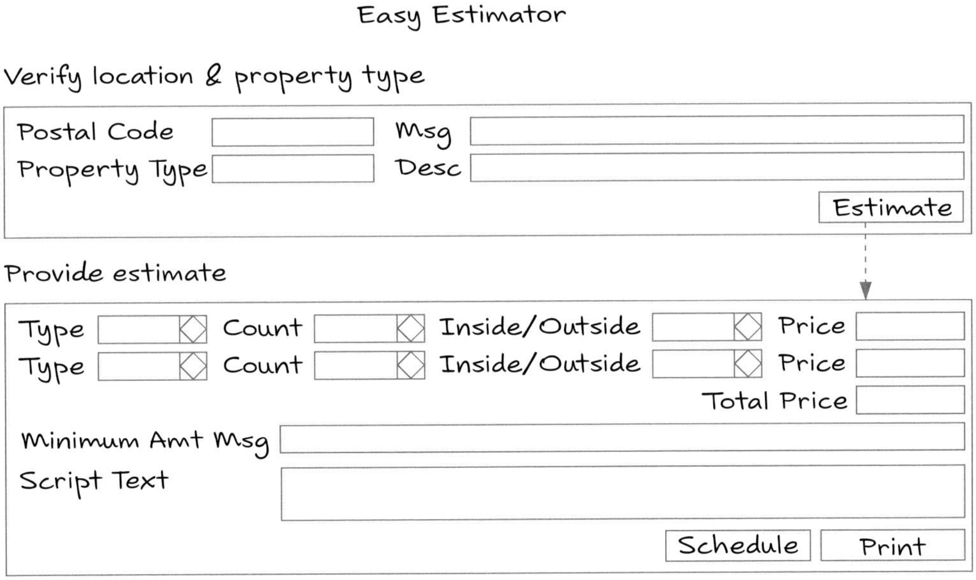

Ted: Right at the top of the prototype we've got postal code. If customers are looking for services that aren't within SK's currently supported areas, we don't want to spend any more time with them.

Ben: Maybe this is a good time to mention *usability* testing?

Ted: Yes. Pat and Ray, we'll want to have a few of the CSRs evaluate the paper prototype and give us early feedback on the look and feel. Ideally we'll get CSRs with a range of skills and experience to try it out.

Deb: I'm concerned. Ray and Ted's drawings show that Easy Estimator will enable the CSR to navigate to scheduling. But we haven't built that capability yet.

Ted: Sorry, we were just envisioning the future. I'll remove it from the next sketch.

Deb: And what about the print capability?

Ted: Again, we're anticipating. We know that some customers might like to have the estimate printed and sent to them by email or fax. Yet realistically, the printed version must include additional information such as the date. These *requirements* go way beyond our goals for the immediate time horizon. I'll remove "Print" from the next sketch. Thanks for keeping us focused, Deb.

Ray: Okay, can we clarify what you will be delivering in the next few weeks? I'm particularly interested in knowing if you're going to include any online tools to help CSRs when they run into trouble with an estimate. For example, the customer can't clearly describe the type of window they want cleaned, and the CSR doesn't know what to do. Can a senior CSR be conferenced in to the call and see the estimating window, or something like that?

Lee: How often does something like this happen? If it's frequent, we need to deal with that sooner rather than later.

Ray: Based on my observations, it happens fairly often.

Deb: Sure, we could provide some software help—but that would change my estimate to deliver the story to a Large. What about exploring some non-automated solutions? Then we can compare the alternatives—the financial costs, both short term and long term, balanced against the benefits. Remember: adding more software features means we'd need to consider the cost of delay in providing some immediate relief for the majority of the estimates. This may sound very simplistic, but could a short-term approach be changing where the CRSs sit—maybe pairing an experienced CSR next to a less experienced CSR?

Pat: Great ideas, Deb. Let's add this topic to our research list. I want to know more specifics, like how frequently this happens, what the customer questions are, what impact it has in training CSRs. Ted, can you work with Ray and me to explore this situation?

Ted: Sure.

Ben: Maybe this is a good time to look at some *examples*. Ray has pulled together three recent, typical estimates. Ray, can you pass those out?

The team pauses and reviews the examples. Lee asks about the postal code on the examples.

Pat: We use the postal code for two things. Like Ted said, the first thing we do is verify that we offer services in the requested location. That's pretty easy. The other thing has to do with looking up tax percentages—sales tax—so we can calculate the tax and add it to the price estimate. In the locations we currently service, there's only one tax. But when we start our franchising initiative, we expect that some locations may have multiple taxes—for example, a city tax as well as a regional tax.

Deb: Whoa! This is complicated! Estimating the tax amount raises the size of this story to Extra Large. Is it really necessary to include the taxes in the estimate now?

Pat: I hear you. Okay, to keep with our Easy Estimator theme, I'll settle for calculating the price of the services. But we must clearly communicate to the customers that the estimated price does not include taxes.

Ted: This is another opportunity to add "scriptlike" information to the CSR's screen. I'll need the standard language from you, Pat—or is it Sales?

Pat: I'll work with Sales to get the text.

Ted: I need to know more about the types of things that can be estimated. For this release we're limiting estimates to just cleaning residential windows.

Ray's examples show many different types—double-hung, casement, tilt-in, half-moons, picture, transom. The number of unique types will impact the design and usability of the interface.

Ray: I can get you a full list. This brings up another opportunity to help the CSRs be more effective and efficient. From my own initial experience helping new-hire CSRs, it's, uh, challenging to get them fluent in the different window types. How is a double-hung window different from a transom window? Remember Roger, our persona for a customer? He doesn't want to feel ignorant when we ask him how many windows of a particular type he wants cleaned. But he doesn't know the lingo. So a few years ago I created a cheat sheet. It has drawings of the different types of windows, and a little description of each one. It helped me during my first few months, and since then I've shared it with new hires. A lot of them have added their own notes and tips.

Pat: Ray, I didn't realize you originated that sheet—thank you! It's been a real asset. Maybe now is the time to take it to the next generation. Can we compile everybody's notes and tips and come up with a single, comprehensive version? It would be an accurate, clearly written "job aid" (she makes air quotes) that the CSRs can reference as they talk with customers. It could list each window type, along with a text description and an image.

Ben: I'd be glad to help with that. Should we include those details in the Easy Estimator application's first release?

Ted: Hold on a minute. Once you've got the version you want, let's look at the impact on UI design and usability. We need to balance serving the needs of the experienced CSRs like you, Ray, who really know this stuff, and the less experienced CSRs, who don't. Adding this level of detail to the UI could lead to a lot of clicking or scrolling to get past the drawings, and that would slow the experienced users down. This could have a direct, negative impact on achieving our objective "90% of the estimates provided by the Easy Estimator application will be completed in less than 3 minutes."

Deb: The interface we need to build now is for the CSRs' frequent use—many times a day. The UI could include a standard description to help the CSRs provide an estimate. But I'm not sure the CSRs need to see the picture of the window type on their screen. On the other hand, if we roll out the customer version of Easy Estimator, we might want to show an image and description for each type to ensure a more accurate estimate. Also, it could reduce calls asking for clarification about window types.

Ben: Let's get back to our immediate need—the CSRs—before I have to yellow-card you (he smiles). We have two—make that three—options. One, the most complete, integrated solution would be to extend the estimating application to include images and text descriptions of every window type we service. Two, the simplest and fastest approach is to give each CSR a paper version of Ray's revised Window Description job aid. And three, somewhere in the middle, is scanning the Window Description text and loading it on the CSRs' computers for easy reference.

The team discusses these options. Pat notes that the complete, integrated approach would be very beneficial for the CSRs, but she doesn't want to risk a delay in delivering Easy Estimator. The spring cleaning season is around the corner, and three new CSRs are starting work next month. She makes a decision.

Pat: Let's start with the simple approach. Ray, can you and Ben draft the revised Window Description job aid and then send it to Sarah in Sales? We need her to review and update it as needed. (Ray nods.) Ted, can you review it as well for usability? I remember you said that even a paper reference document has usability aspects. We want to be sure the CSRs can visually scan it and quickly find details they might need on a call with a customer. Make sense?

Ted: Yes, there are definitely usability aspects to a written document, and we can test those. For example, how long does it take a junior CSR to find a specific window type description? That reference document will be the starting point for content and design layout when we add it to the online Easy Estimator application.

Pat: Good. Also, for this first delivery of Easy Estimator, I want Deb and Ted to find a way to link to the text descriptions. That way, we'll have a standard vocabulary for the CSRs to use when they're on the phone with customers.

Ben: I like this approach. We can iteratively deliver small slices to improve CSR effectiveness and learn as we go. First a paper version, next some limited text online, then images online. At each point we can assess the value and make adjustments accordingly.

Deb: Right. We can experiment with a few designs for the description and images.

Ted: And we can do some usability testing with Ray to decide, within a few hours, which is better.

Pat: And how about one or two junior CRSs as well?

Ted: Absolutely.

Deb: You know, ideally we can repurpose and reuse a lot of the code when we create a version of Easy Estimator for direct use by customers. That's an important technology value we have.

Ted: Yes, to some extent I agree with you, Deb. But I just want to point out that we'll have to rework the interface design to serve another audience—the customers. They're not frequent users like the CSRs.

Ben: (Holding up his yellow index card.) Let's regroup here. Our immediate need is a simple user interface for the CSRs. Let's be sure to stay in scope for the Now-View.

Pat: Thanks, Ben. That said, I appreciate you all for not losing sight of the Big-View. (She smiles.) Thanks for keeping the Options board up-to-date throughout our conversation. I want to take it all in so we can make some decisions.

Together the team members review the Options board. They consider which high-value options they can deliver in the first iteration. They assemble sets of options into small, cohesive chunks, each of which provides value individually and collectively. They write a story to reflect the scope:

> As a CSR Estimator, I need to (verbally) provide on off-site cleaning estimate (excluding taxes and discounts) for a standard residential property's windows, so the customer can decide whether to use SK's services.

Ben sketches a context diagram to represent the story.

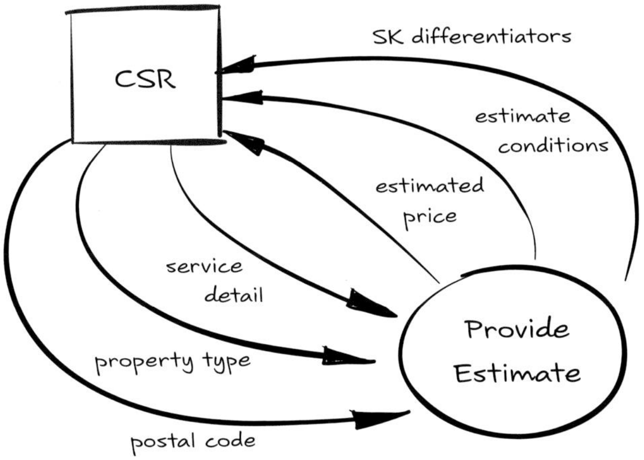

Now-View: Out of the Blocks

High-value options are noted with a star (*)

	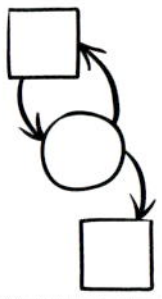	
User	Interface	Action
Estimator Role* CSR* CSR state* Junior*	Customer to CSR* request details verbal * CSR to Customer* estimate verbal* printed CSR to-from the application* UI*	Provide estimate* verify requested location* select window type* display window type description display window type image enter count of window type* calculate window type subtotal price* calculate total window type estimated price* apply coupon apply discount calculate tax amount calculate total estimated price* compare estimate to minimum* communicate estimate to customer* print estimate send printed estimate to customer
Sales Manager*	Manager to the application Manual UI	Manage service data* capture service data add service data update service data delete service data communicate service data to staff*
Note: This area of the Options board is used for models.		

Options Board

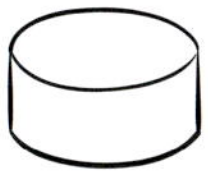 Data	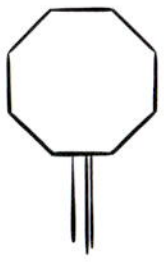 Control	 Environment	 Quality Attribute
Coupon Discount Estimate* window type count* total window type estimated price* total estimated price* Location* postal code* tax percentage Property type* residential standard* Service* cleaning* Service area* postal code* effective date Window type* name* description cleaning price* image	Estimate is an approximate price* Non-standard property services must be estimated on-site* Total window type price = (window type count x price)* Total estimated price = sum of total window type price* Minimum price for providing service is $60* Only an authorized Sales person must add, change or delete service details	SK Office* Database* BigBox Relational ElephantOpen SourceDataStorage* Browser* greatBrowser3.2 and above iAmBrowser7.2 and above* Operating Systems* Penguin BigSoft* Upstart GreatScripting lan-guage 7.0 – to be confirmed* Farmers4Application Servers*	Usability* Amount of time to provide estimate with no help, based on average of 10 estimate requests (for 3 or fewer window types), final estimated price and service items communicated within 2 minutes* Availability* 98% during regular SK business hours* Performance* Subtotal price displays on screen within 1 second after entering number of windows*

Due to space limitations the models are not shown.
See www.DiscoverToDeliver.com for samples.

Next, the partners discuss dependencies. The dependency identified in the Pre-View session needs to be addressed now: providing an estimate is dependent on having the current service details readily available. Pat has been clear that Sales owns that data. Ben shares that he talked with Sarah yesterday and updated the "service" *data domain*. He points to the changes on the Options board.

The team discusses how to get the data into the Easy Estimator app. They learn that the service area and window type description data changes infrequently; for example, the prices are reviewed semiannually but typically are changed only once a year. Even though one of the team's objectives is to enable the Sales folks to enter changes directly into Easy Estimator, Deb and Lee suggest that for this two-week delivery cycle, the data can be hard-coded into the application. Pat agrees to defer the objective for the time being. Speed is of the essence to meet the other objectives.

As a CSR,
I need a window cleaning reference sheet to use when estimating,
so I can provide descriptions of window types and the exact wording of SK cleaning policies.

In the following iteration, they will build a simple interface to enable Sales to quickly and independently add, update, and delete all service and window type details. They'll populate it with the existing data and do some usability testing. Once that's working, they will update the Easy Estimator to use that data.

Ted draws a context diagram to visualize the interfaces needed to manage the service data.

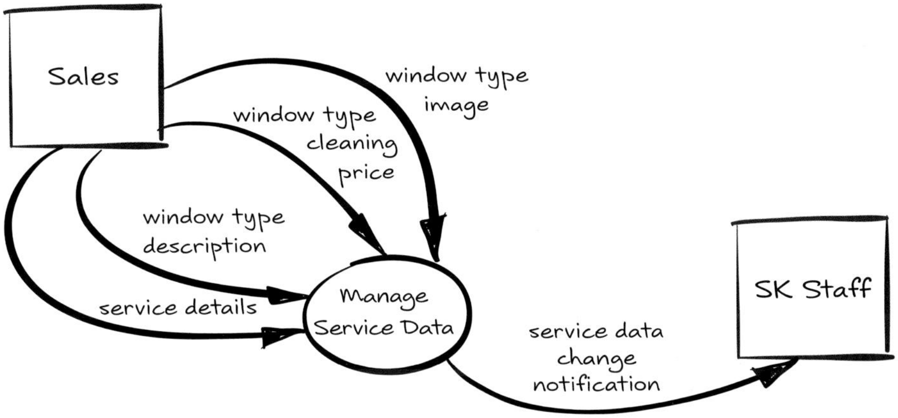

Lee and Deb ask Pat to clarify the scope. Pat goes over to the context diagram on the Options board and uses a highlighter to select the high-value interfaces: service details, window type description, and window type cleaning price. The image and change notification interfaces will have to wait.

> Ben: Okay. Let's take a short break. When we reconvene I'll have a few scenarios for the Provide Estimate story. We can use these scenarios to confirm our understanding. These examples will feed our *acceptance criteria* down the road.

Alone in the room, Ben jots down the scenarios:

Customer requests services for a property in an area that SK does not currently service

Customer requests cleaning services for commercial property

Customer requests cleaning services for non-standard residential window type

Estimated total price equals or exceeds SK minimum price

Estimated total price is less than SK minimum price

When the team returns, they review the scenarios and agree they're a good start. Deb and Ben offer to write *data examples* to serve as acceptance criteria for the candidate solutions. They will confirm the data with Pat and Ray.

Deb: Now let's do some estimating.

After some discussion the team agrees that Provide Estimate is now a small-sized story. They're confident they can develop it and have a few rounds of usability testing with the CSRs within the upcoming release. Depending on their *work-in-progress limits*, they'll *pull* stories from the backlog in the priority order that Pat has indicated.

The Structured Conversation Wrap Up

The team agrees to arrange their *workflow board* after lunch. It will include work-in-progress limits along with lanes and rows to visualize who is doing what work. The board will also show recommended practices for handling the interruptions that sometimes arise from technical support issues once they begin supporting the product in production.

Ben guides the team in their quick check to confirm they've covered all the bases:

- They observed and analyzed the business work that needs to be improved.
- Their decisions have been grounded in the value considerations of all partners, balancing benefits, risks, dependencies, and the estimates to develop.
- They addressed each of the 7 Product Dimensions throughout the conversation (and used models when helpful).
- They actively worked on the glossary.

Pat: I'm really pleased with what we've gotten done today. I'm going to review these stories and scenarios with a few of the junior CSRs to make sure we haven't missed anything.

In the meantime, they agree:

- Pat will check with Sales for current window types, descriptions, and prices.
- Pat will work with Sales on a script to describe the window types and will review it with Ray and one junior CSR.

- Pat will get final approval for the SK estimating policies script from Sales.
- Lee will confirm they have the software development tools for building Easy Estimator.
- Ben and Deb will write acceptance criteria for the stories.

As is their custom, the team concludes the planning session with a retrospective. To begin, they review the retrospective Learning Points poster from the Pre-View session. After discussion, they write the following on a poster:

- Continue starting with a narrow scope.
- It's helpful to have Ray (the "voice of the user") engaged in the session.
- Using real examples helps us drill down into details.
- Continue to do retrospectives.
- Rotate the retrospective facilitator role for planning sessions in the next release.

The Next Day

Ben and Deb show the team some ideas for acceptance criteria.

Scenario	Example	Expected result
Customer requests service for a property in an area that SK does not currently service	Area: 22235	Message: SK does not currently provide services in that area
Customer requests cleaning services for commercial property	Property type: commercial property	Message: SK does not currently service commercial properties
Customer requests cleaning services for non-standard residential windows	Window type: non-standard	Message: To provide an accurate price estimate, we need to do an on-site survey of your property
Estimated total price equals or exceeds minimum price	Total estimated amount: $85	Estimate is displayed Standard language is displayed
Estimated total price does not meet SK's minimum price	Total estimated amount: $55	Message: The total price for the requested services does not meet SK's minimum price

Pat points to the third scenario. She'd like the message to end with: "Would you like to schedule an appointment for an on-site visit?" It is more customer-friendly and better for SK too. For the last scenario's message she requests they add, "Would you like to add any services to reach the minimum price?" She explains that it might result in the customer deciding to use more of SK's services.

Ben and Deb promise to add the text. They describe how they will elaborate the scenarios in a series of *Given-When-Thens*. The team agrees that this will be a great way to both *verify* and *validate* each iteration within a release.

The First Big-View Planning and Analysis Session

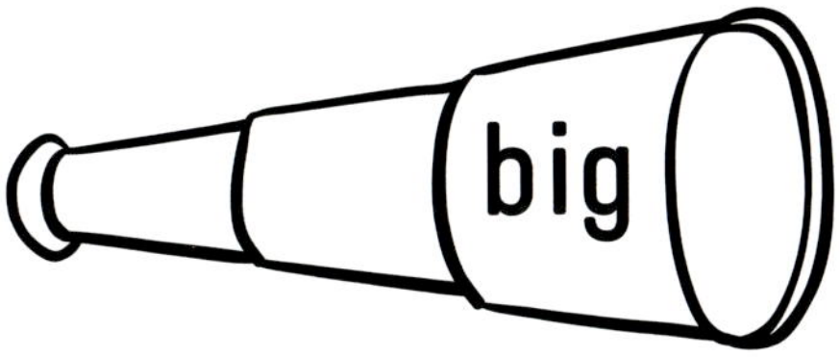

The Partners

The product partners come from the business, customer, and technology community. The people who are present for this first Big-View planning session are noted with a star (*).

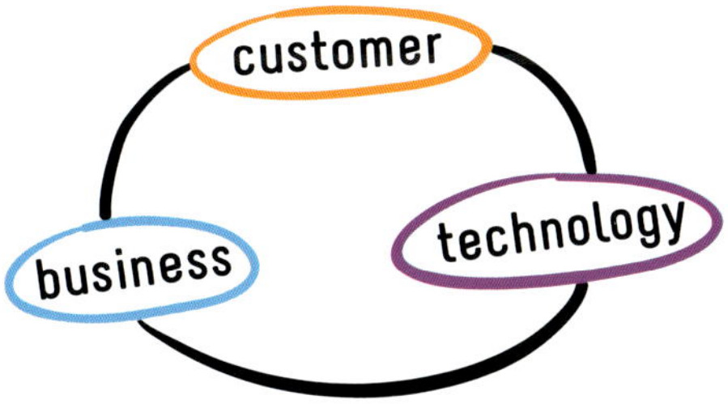

SK Business Partners
- Sal, Squeeky Kleen CEO, Sponsor*
- SK management team
  - Frank, Finance and Inventory*
  - Pat, SK Office Manager, Product Champion*
  - Sarah, Sales Manager*

SK Customer Partners
- Squeeky Kleen customers and office staff, users

Apps-R-Us Technology Partners
- Lee, Information Architecture and Development*
- Ben, Planning and Analysis*
- Deb, Development
- Ted, User Experience and Testing

Preparation: Before the Session

While the product team worked on the Easy Estimator, SK's management team prepared for its Big-View session. The managers reviewed and revised their business model, updated the SK glossary, and conducted additional market research and a competitive analysis. They also investigated cost structures to support their value proposition for expanding the business, studied the implications of internationalization, and looked into options for potential strategic partners—including builders and real estate agents.

Sal worked with the management team to clarify SK's overall vision: "To be a trusted partner for reliable, safe, and competitively priced cleaning." They agreed to pursue four goals:

- Increase revenue from the residential business.
- Protect revenue and reputation by complying with local regulations.
- Obtain efficiencies in estimating and scheduling.
- Add new revenues by moving into new services (such as repairs), new markets (including commercial cleaning), and franchises across the country and then internationally.

Sal often dropped by the product team room to check progress on the Easy Estimator application and occasionally to observe work sessions. He and the other managers were impressed by the visual power of the team's Options board as well as the team's workflow board.

Sal noticed that the team members used their Options board continually to illustrate the current state of their structured conversations and depict the possibilities and decisions they'd considered for the various product options. The team was continually adding and removing items; coloring, highlighting, starring, and crossing out items; and posting sketches of analysis models.

Sal also noticed that the product team used the Options board in building its queue for the Now-View work. He decided the Options board could be helpful to the management team as it worked to explore and evaluate options for SK's Big-View.

The management team, with help from Ted and Ben, created several scenarios to describe the end-to-end journey a persona might experience based on the SK vision. Here is one example:

> Roger Smith has just purchased a new property and needs help getting it cleaned. He checks with Squeeky Kleen to learn about its services and get an estimate. A few days later Roger calls back to schedule the cleaning work. After the job is completed, Squeeky Kleen bills Roger for the services. When his payment is received, a Squeeky Kleen representative follows up with Roger to make sure he is satisfied and to offer him a discount coupon for future services.

The partners also researched and agreed on the following Big-View value considerations:

Customer Value Considerations

- Reasonable cost, reliable, "I can trust you on my property"
- Request the same cleaner
- Feel good about using safe cleaning products
- Convenient to use SK for a variety of services in a variety of ways
- Good investment in my property, discounts, competitive prices.

Business Value Considerations

- Align with vision
- Leader in the market
- Brand projection
- Cross-sell services
- Productivity of all employees
- Safety of cleaners
- Grow business in sustainable, ethical manner.

Technology Value Considerations

- Comply with common architecture
- Frequent delivery to accelerate technical learning
- Build for future expansion
- Foundation for efficient support and enhancements
- Platform that can interface with external providers.

Summary of The Structured Conversation

The management team, along with Ben and Lee, meets to make important decisions. The partners explore product options for scheduling cleaning and repair jobs as well as options dealing with inventory, reporting, accounting and payroll, partnerships, and sales and marketing. The scenarios they prepared earlier enrich the conversation.

They consider users, including employees in finance, sales, and marketing as well as customers. They discuss interface options and the wide variety of mobile computing possibilities, as well as interfaces to external systems. The data options include Inventory, Employee, Estimate, Job, Account, Marketing Campaign, and more. This leads to their exploring business policies such as union implications, *regulations* for access to commercial buildings, and insurance and bonding.

They look at *quality attributes* for the candidate solutions; they quickly grasp how important *performance*, usability, and scalability will be in meeting their vision. They discuss options for the operational and development environments. With Lee's leadership they review the team's technology roadmap.

The management team evaluates all the options listed on the Big-View Options board and aligns them with SK's vision and goals. They assemble the high-value options into features and determine the impact of their value considerations on the features' benefits and risks. They weight these factors, along with dependencies, to collectively arrive at value decisions that became the basis for creating the *product roadmap*. They agree that before SK moves into servicing commercial properties, the product team will focus on sustaining and gaining customers in the residential property market. The management team also agrees that SK needs better accounting systems to support its expected growth. The partners plan to clarify accounting options and are open to purchasing and integrating a packaged software solution.

The Structured Conversation Wrap Up

The SK management team pauses to conduct a retrospective of their planning session, reflecting on their group process and deciding what worked and what might be improved for future sessions. Improvements include defining ways to improve their preparation for these complex planning sessions. They wrap up by agreeing to schedule a walkthrough of their outcomes with the entire product team. They agree they need to continually tune their plans using feedback from the iterative and incremental delivery of the candidate solutions. They will review and revise the product roadmap using this validated learning.

Big-View Plan

Theme	Easy Estimator	Trust Me
Release	1	2
Candidate Solutions	Off-site cleaning estimates Self-service hypothesis (24x7) Customer history conversion Automatic supply replenishment	Optimize scheduling Self-service cleaning estimates On-site cleaning estimates Cleaner-customer profile matching Media outreach Sparkling Home Discount program

Product Roadmap

Show Me the Money	Grow Up	Big Box
3	4	5
Self-service scheduling Repair service hypothesis Instant pay Accounting package Search engine optimization Scale servers and networks	Franchise Online training Repair service estimates & scheduling Inventory optimization Performance and throughput optimization Real estate agent referrals	Commercial property hypothesis Internationalize franchises

Section 2

BIG CONCEPTS

BIG CONCEPTS

Discover to Deliver™

Agile/Lean software development teams evolve products through the ongoing, interwoven activities of *discovery* and delivery.

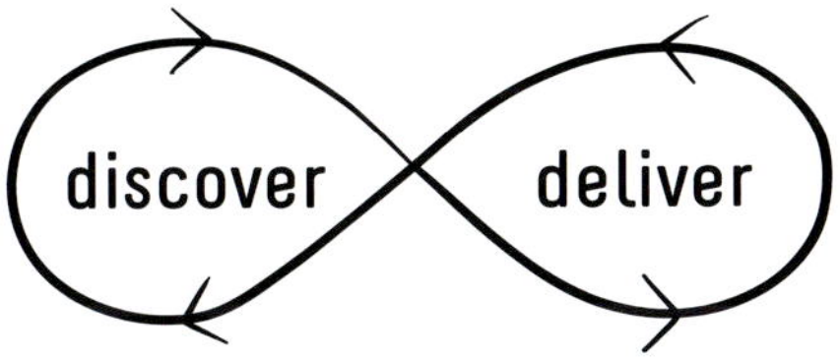

Product

To create a *product*, you identify and build the *product options* that will provide value.

The Product

As you discover and deliver each product option, you look at it in terms of the 7 Product Dimensions.

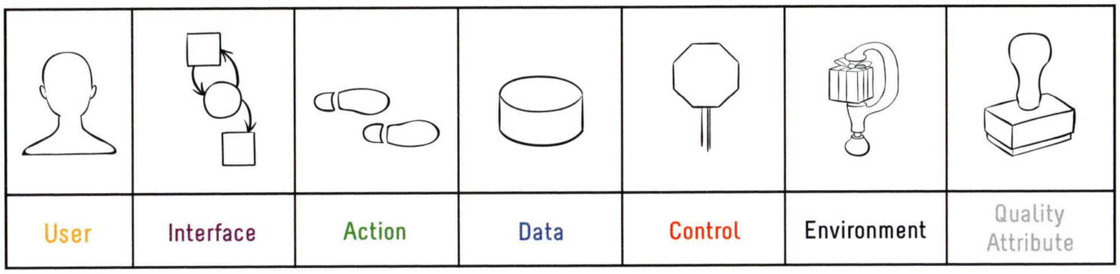

The 7 Product Dimensions

Product Partnership

Customers, business people, and technology experts form and sustain a *partnership*. These three types of *partners* collaborate throughout product discovery and delivery.

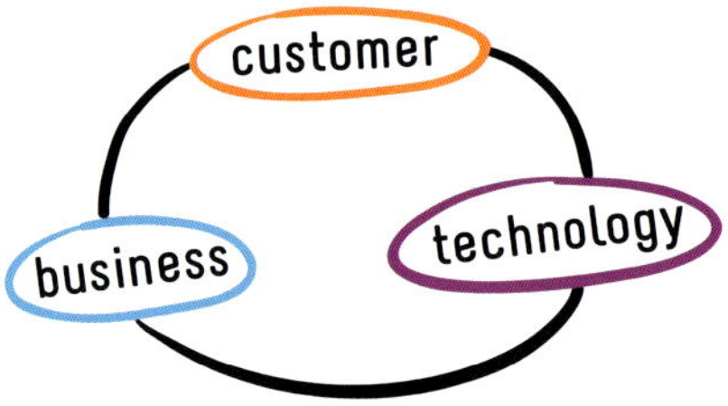

Product partners fall into three groups

Value

You identify the *value* you seek from each product option, and that value drives your planning as you discover and deliver the product. Value is the end, and the product options are the means, to obtain this value. Each product option presents benefits and risks, and you assess these as part of determining the option's value.

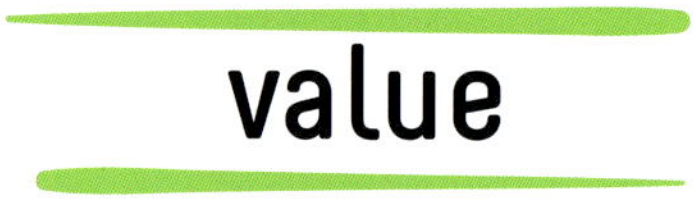

To assess a product option, the partners determine its value

Plan

You allocate the chosen product options to a *plan*.

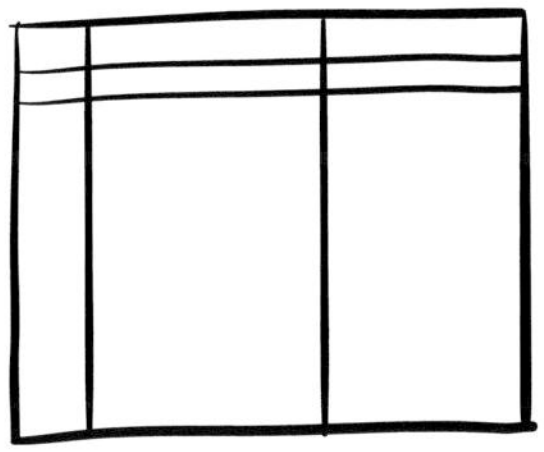

The partners create a plan for delivering the product options

You use three *planning views*, or time horizons.

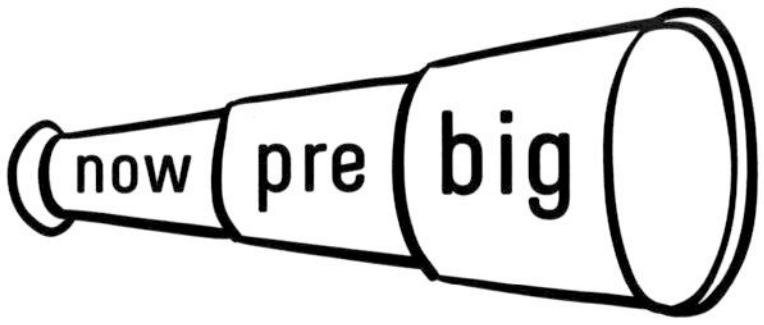

Three planning views are useful for planning

Structured Conversation

You use the structured conversation for ongoing, systematic, and collaborative discovery and delivery of product options.

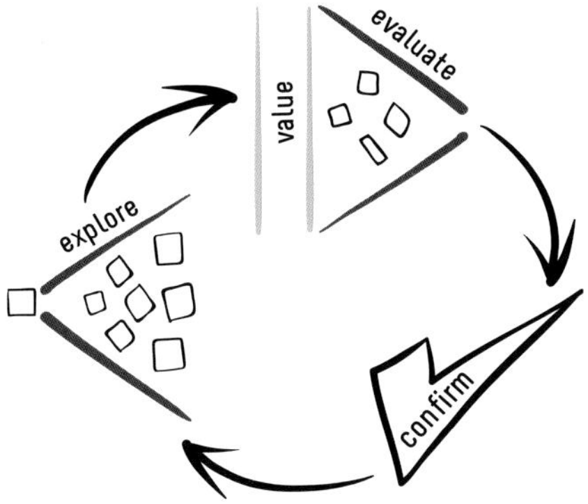

The Structured Conversation

Product

A product provides value to stakeholders.

A product is a software application, system, or device containing software that provides value to customers and business partners. The product may be created for internal or external use. It may be software or may be a system composed of hardware and software.

How do you discover and prepare product options? How do you make sure you have a holistic view of the product? How can you be sure you're building the right product?

A product is the result of many decisions you make throughout discovery and delivery—decisions that are driven by feedback from partial implementation and continual delivery.

Product Types

You can develop your product using a variety of means. If it's an internal product, it might be developed by your IT (information technology) group, an external party, or some combination; or you might acquire it as a packaged solution (e.g., COTS, or commercial off-the-shelf, software), which you might configure for your organization. You may develop an external product for sale to other organizations or consumers, or you might develop it under contract with an external technology partner.

Vision: Source for the Product

A *product vision* is the long-term concept of the product. The vision outlines the product's key benefit or purpose as well as its differentiators and advantages. The vision explains how the product contributes to your organization's strategy. The product must have value so that buyers will be willing to exchange money, time, or some other resource for it. The vision itself may evolve over time, as the organization or its business needs evolve, or you receive feedback from the market or users.

The 7 Product Dimensions

	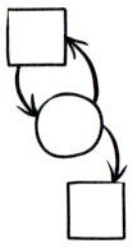		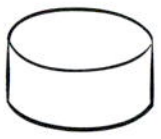			
User	Interface	Action	Data	Control	Environment	Quality Attribute
Users interact with the product	The product connects to users, systems, and devices	The product provides capabilities for users	The product includes a repository of data and useful information	The product enforces constraints	The product conforms to physical properties and technology platforms	The product has certain properties that qualify its operation and development

The 7 Product Dimensions give the partners a holistic, comprehensive understanding of the product. No single dimension, by itself, is sufficient. Throughout ongoing structured conversations, the partners ask:

- What users have goals related to this product?
- What interfaces are needed?
- What actions are needed?
- What data are acted on?
- What controls must be enforced?
- What environments will the product operate in and be developed in?
- What quality attributes constrain and control the product?

These dimensions may be categorized as *functional* (users, actions, data, and controls) and *nonfunctional* (interfaces, environments, and quality attributes). For more about how the 7 Product Dimensions interrelate, see Section 3, The 7 Product Dimensions. For more about how the partners explore, evaluate, and confirm product options, see Section 4, The Structured Conversation.

Discovering Options

Regardless of the initial size of the *product need* —expressed as a feature, *use case*, or story – you use the structured conversation to quickly explore alternatives for the 7 Product Dimensions, uncovering possibilities—options. Each option is a choice for fulfilling the product vision.

You might define product options in various formats, such as stories, one-line titles, story descriptions, and so on. You might add sketches, models, prototypes, examples, tests, and the like. Regardless of how product options are represented, you use all 7 Product Dimensions to efficiently and effectively clarify the options.

As partners, you evaluate the potential product options, identify the highest-value options, and assemble them into cohesive sets—candidate solution. A candidate solution can take different forms. It might be an increment of the product, a prototype, a specific, thinly sliced user story, or even as simple as a partial implementation of an interface with little or no functionality.

Continuous Product Delivery

Over time, the product evolves in functionality and increases in value as additional options are incorporated.

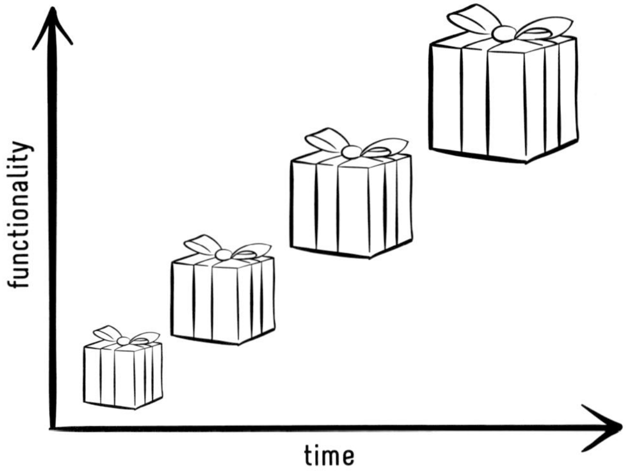

The Product Backlog

Your *product backlog* is a catalog (or queue) containing unrealized product options at varying levels of detail. The *backlog items* are tentative; they don't represent a guarantee of what will be delivered or how it will be delivered. Rather, backlog items represent possibilities for the product.

Some teams include infrastructure, housekeeping, and product packaging items in their backlog. Others integrate those elements into product options.

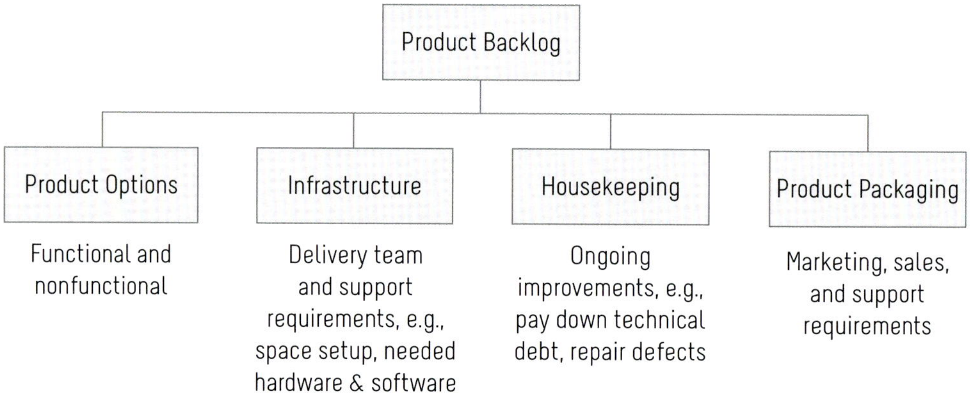

Product Backlog Item Categories

A typical product backlog contains a mix of product options across all three planning views. A healthy product backlog is dynamic, continually evolving as you discover and deliver product options.

Product Backlog Dynamics

As you discover, you continually explore and evaluate options to assemble candidate solutions. You confirm your shared expectations for the candidate solution. Over time the product evolves as candidate solutions are realized.

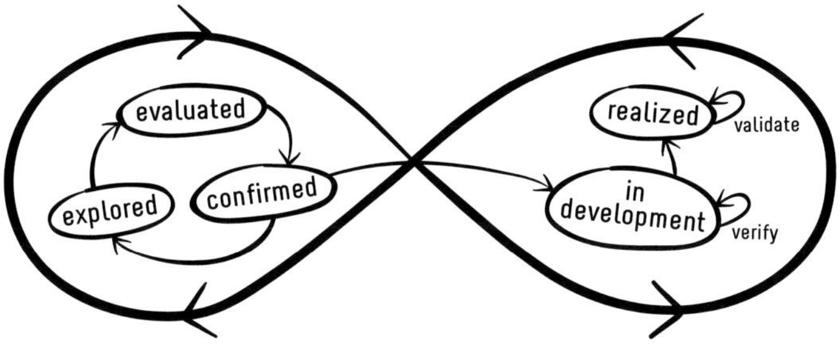

Lifecycle of Backlog Item Diagram

Rather than accumulate and manage a great many possible product options, Agile/Lean teams focus on exploring and choosing the next-highest-value options at any given point in time. In this way, you limit the number and age of backlog items.

Ideally, the life expectancy of most backlog items from discovery to delivery is short. This makes economic sense, because small, lean backlogs (or queues of product development work) enable faster delivery (Anderson 2010, Reinertsen 2009).

The Product Partnership

Product teams explore and evaluate product options and plan development through a partnership of business, customer, and technical stakeholders.

A *stakeholder* is anyone with a stake or interest in the product. Stakeholders may include people from the business side of the organization, technical people, and internal customers, as well as people from outside the organization such as external customers, regulators, or suppliers.

Successful products incorporate the perspectives of diverse stakeholders—what we call the product partnership. Collaborating as partners, these people reach a shared understanding of the product options and decide which options to deliver at a given point in time.

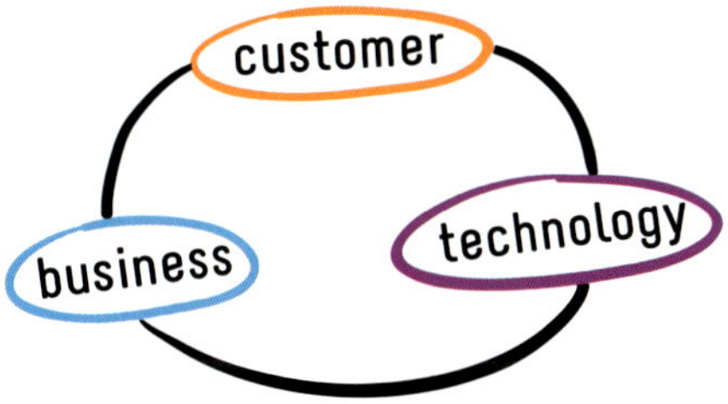

Product Partnership

Who should be in your product partnership? What are their perspectives?
What's the right mix of perspectives for this product?

The product partnership involves various types of people, each with unique perspectives.

Characteristics of the Product Partnership

A good product partnership has these characteristics.

Attitude: The partners envision and deliver a product together, focused on goals and not roles.

Cross-Discipline: The partners offer a mix of disciplines, experience, and viewpoints. They combine their knowledge and capabilities to leverage opportunities and solve problems.

Product Life Cycle Perspective: Partners are engaged during the product's entire life cycle, from discovery through development, deployment, training, maintenance and enhancement, customer and technical support, and retirement. They value each release as the actualization of the unfolding product vision. Post-delivery, the partners confirm that the delivered product options achieved the anticipated value.

Commitment: A stable group of core partners provides consistency and heightened productivity. Specialists may be brought in occasionally to provide specific skills or knowledge.

The Product Champion

The product partnership benefits from having a leader to balance all the perspectives, reconcile differences, and make final decisions about the product. We like to call this partner the product champion; others use the term *product owner*.

This leader is a master of both long-term (strategic) and short-term (tactical) thinking. The product champion may hail from product management (if the product is for commercial sale) or from a line of business (if the product is for internal use). Alternatively, the product champion may be an experienced technologist with deep business *domain* expertise.

In some cases, the product champion role may be filled by two people—typically, a technical architect and a business domain expert. For large, complex products, the product champion may form a product council or advisory group (we recommend no more than seven people) representing cross-functional perspectives.

Product Partner Types

Customer Partner Roles	Example Motivations
User • Interacts with the product to achieve the product's stated goals • May be a human, an interfacing system, or a hardware device • Includes support users (e.g., help desk staffers, installers, operators, trainers)	• Give me a satisfying experience • Don't slow me down • Enable my work • Entertain me • Help me self-actualize
Buyer • Purchases product	• Enhance my bottom line • Give my users a satisfying experience
Adviser • Provides guidance about purchasing the product • Influencer, advocate	• Enhance my customer's bottom line

business

Business Partner Roles

Sponsor
- Authorizes, legitimates, or pays for product development or for the purchase of a commercial software product
- For government software, usually a department manager
- For internal IT products, usually a business manager
- Other titles: backer, benefactor, buyer, guarantor, owner, gold owner

Product Champion
- Studies market opportunities
- Identifies high-value customers
- Ensures that the needs of diverse users are satisfied
- Monitors market trends, customer segments
- Articulates a compelling product vision
- Ensures alignment with company strategy and with other products in the portfolio
- For commercial software, usually a product manager
- Other titles: ambassador, product manager, product visionary, product owner

Provider
- Provides products or services that support the product
- Participates in a business-to-business relationship

Adviser
- Provides vital business information about the product
- Shares knowledge of policies and regulations
- Includes subject matter experts in audit, change management, finance, legal, human resources, operational support, process design experience, training, sales and marketing, etc.

Example Motivations

- Realize my business case
- Maintain or improve my market position
- Protect my revenue
- Comply with regulations (e.g., human safety, financial, privacy, environmental)

- Keep or increase my user base
- Ensure my market viability and timeliness
- Increase my customers' satisfaction, reduce my customers' displeasure
- Meet or beat the market trends

- Keep or increase my partners' satisfaction
- Achieve my own business case

- Enhance our organization's performance

technology

Technology Partner Roles

Builder

- Designs, builds, buys, tests, deploys, delivers, supports the product; referred to as the delivery team
- Internal or third-party vendor
- Includes architects, business analysts, data and database administrators, developers, installers, operations staffers, testers, training and help desk staffers, user experience experts, etc.

Adviser

- Provides vital product information: implementation, information technology, governance and compliance, installation, operational support, technical architecture, training
- Includes subject matter experts: auditors, operators, trainers, etc.

Example Motivations

Builder:

- Offer a high-quality software product
- Offer smooth, continual delivery of product value

Adviser:

- Share my knowledge of rules and regulations

Value

A product delivers value when it provides a fair return in exchange for time, money, goods, or services.

A successful product delivers value that is aligned with the product's vision and *goals*. You make product decisions at every turn throughout discovery and delivery based on value, balancing multiple considerations and perspectives.

Value can change depending on timing, market demand, and emerging technologies. You assess product value continually. Post-delivery, you compare the actual value achieved to the anticipated value to determine whether the objectives have been achieved.

value

What do you want in this product? How can you identify the most valuable options? What might threaten product value? Heighten value?

The partners use value to evaluate options.

Desirable and Feasible

Valuable products are both desirable and feasible.

Desirability is the worth or utility of the product to stakeholders.

Feasibility is the realistic expectation of success given your financial, technical, market, and organizational constraints. Feasibility is about being able to build the product at a price that will return the desired tangible and intangible results.

Tangible and Intangible

Value can be tangible and easy to measure, such as increasing or protecting revenues or reducing operating costs. Or value might be more intangible and difficult to measure, such as enhancing the product's likeability and convenience.

When you deliver a product that satisfies the customers' stated and implied needs, you can reap many benefits. When you fail to deliver a customer-satisfying product, you suffer numerous risks.

Ends and Means

Ends are the desired outcomes expressed in the product's vision, goals, and objectives. Ends are ways to describe and quantify a product option's anticipated value.

A goal is a target result and is quantified by objectives. An objective is a specific measure that quantifies the goals (ideally SMART: Specific, Measurable, Attainable, Realistic, and Time-based). Together, the vision, goals, and objectives represent the ends—something the organization seeks to accomplish.

Means deliver the desired ends. Ends are neutral of "how" the product is discovered and delivered.

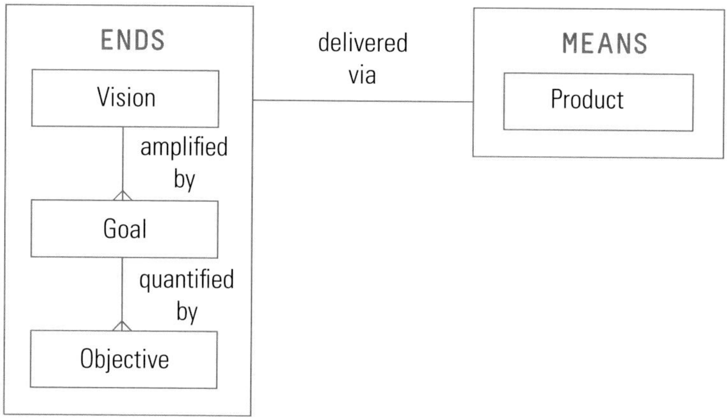

End and Means

Value Is in the Eye of the Beholder

The partners have differing perspectives on value. To arrive at optimal product delivery choices, you need to consider all three perspectives—customer, business, and technology. You can't achieve value without focusing on the customer. Customers value a product for numerous reasons. For example, it solves their problems, it is pleasing to use, or it secures their personal information. Or a customer might value a product that provides a positive visceral reaction, a feeling of enhanced self-worth, or self-actualization.

The user and the buyer may have differing perspectives of the product's value.

A handy tool for exploring a product option's value is IRACIS (pronounced "ear ras cuss"). (Adapted from Gane and Sarson, 1979)

IR: Increase revenue—provide new or enhanced products that people want to buy, and protect existing revenue streams.

AC: Avoid costs (or loss)—reduce expenses and protect revenue.

- Avoid operating costs by introducing operational efficiencies (e.g., reducing delays, duplication, rework, and other forms of waste).
- Avoid penalties due to regulatory violations or adverse events.
- Avoid cost of delay in going to market.
- Avoid lost revenue due to not having competitive features.

IS: Improve service—deliver higher quality, such as greater accuracy, speed, or usability.

Additional factors may be required in your assessment of value. For example, the organization may be less concerned about cost implications and more focused on defining a value-driven cost structure. And intangible value, such as gaining customer trust or learning new technologies, may also be in play.

Value Considerations

A value consideration is a variable used to assess the value of an option. All three types of partners have value considerations.

In addition to revenue, value considerations may incorporate broader values around the context of product usage, design elements, market differentiation, learning, long-term product serviceability, and more.

customer	Personal, Visceral: Convenience Cost, conversion, learning: Cost savings Usage: Physical environment
business	Alignment and Readiness: Align with vision, goals, objectives Differentiation: Market fit, Competitive positioning Cost, Time, Revenue Protection: Cost of delay Expertise: Expertise to discover, install, train, and service the product
technology	Alignment and Readiness: Readiness of technical infrastructure (full, partial, not at all), technical feasibility Cost and Time: Reduce future cost to service Quality Attributes: Data quality, integrity, synchronization Expertise: Expertise to design, build, transition, deliver, install, train, and service the product

Sample Value Considerations

Evaluation: Weighing Benefits and Risks

The partners continually make value decisions about product options. They synthesize multiple factors – their value considerations, benefits, and risks.

Benefits favorably impact the product's value. They provide positive outcomes for the partners. For example, customers might value the benefits of saving time or enjoying an appealing look and feel. The business partners might value financial gains, improved customer loyalty and trust, and enhancements to their customers' bottom line. Technology partners might look at the benefits of leveraging existing assets and competencies.

Risks may unfavorably impact a product's value. A customer might consider a product with insufficient support a risk. The business partners might see a risk in delaying delivery of the product. The technology partners might consider the use of unfamiliar technology as a risk.

When you evaluate the potential risks of a product option, you consider each risk's probability and impact. You might choose either to avoid a risk or to take actions to mitigate it. In some cases there might be value in exploiting a risk. Taking a risk might result in a favorable outcome, even in increased value.

The result of evaluation is a decision on what to build—a candidate solution. The decision aligns with the ends (the product's vision, goals, and objectives).

A candidate solution might be more or less robust, depending on whether the market and the product are new or mature. If the partners are confident their candidate solution will deliver value, they are more likely to deliver a more robust version of the solution. On the other hand, if the candidate solution is innovative or the partners are less certain of the outcomes, they may choose to minimize their investment by delivering a less costly candidate solution such as a prototype, demonstration, or partial implementation of the candidate solution.

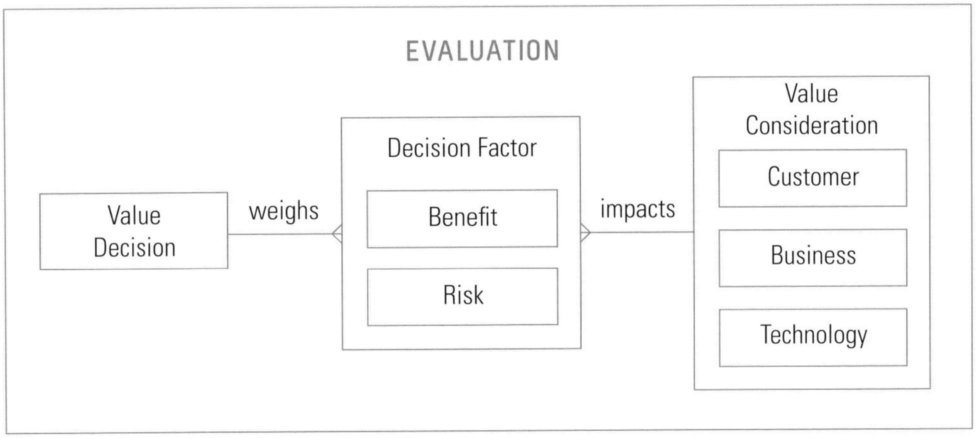

Validated Learning

The product's ends—goals and objectives—are assumptions, not certainties.

Did customers perceive greater convenience or enjoyment (customers' values)? Did the business acquire more customers or reduce operating costs (business values)? Was the product developed with good use of existing technology assets or did the development team learn how to use new, innovative technologies that will increase its technical capabilities (technology values)?

Wise business and technology partners need evidence that the delivered product actually realizes its goals and objectives. They compare the assumptions with post-delivery actual results. This validation provides feedback that is essential for continual learning. The learning helps the partners as they evolve the product.

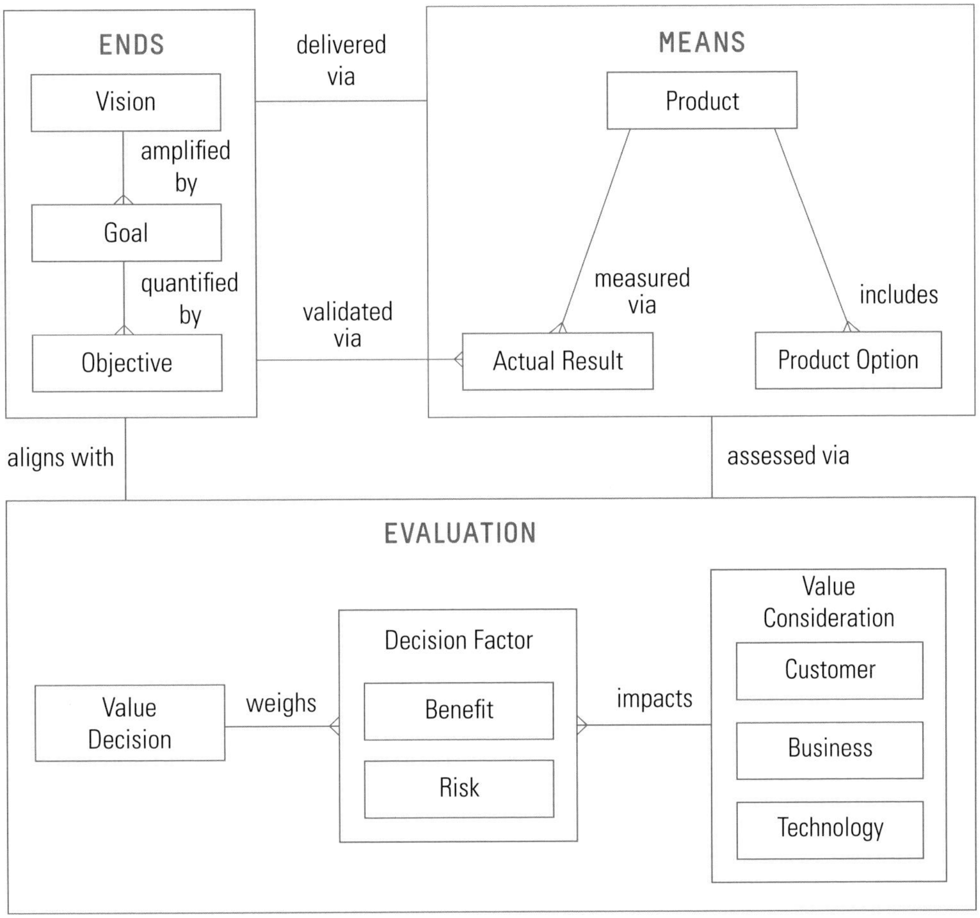

Business Value Model

Plans

A plan represents the partners' allocation of candidate solutions to time horizons.

Plans are the partners' best estimates of what might be delivered during a given *planning horizon* to achieve value. Plans are used to assign funding and to allocate people and resources to product development.

A planning horizon—the period of time that the plan covers—might be strategic (such as a plan for the entire product or product portfolio) or tactical (for immediate delivery). As you continually discover, deliver, and evaluate the product, your planning improves.

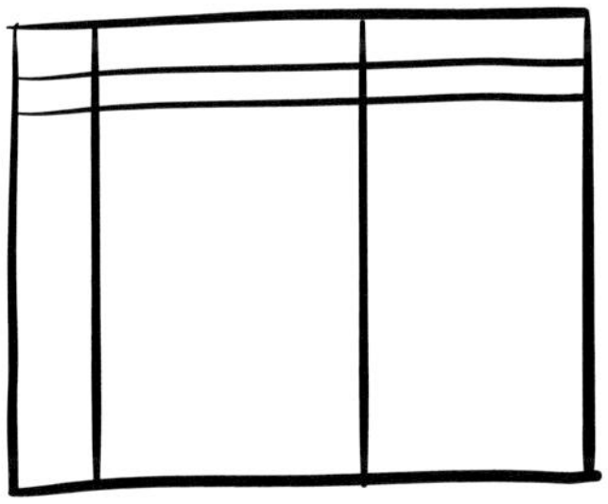

Plans

What are plan time horizons? What level of detail is appropriate for your plans? What is the basis for plans?

The team creates various plans, and the granularity varies depending on the planning view.

The Three Planning Views

As you hold continual, value-driven conversations, each product option evolves, often transitioning through all three planning views in its lifetime.

A product option may start as a general idea—such as a feature that will fulfill some aspect of the product vision. As time passes, it is explored, evaluated, and reevaluated, and it may eventually be allocated for delivery. The product option gets more fine-grained (detailed) as you descend the planning view hierarchy. As a result, plans and estimates become increasingly fine-grained.

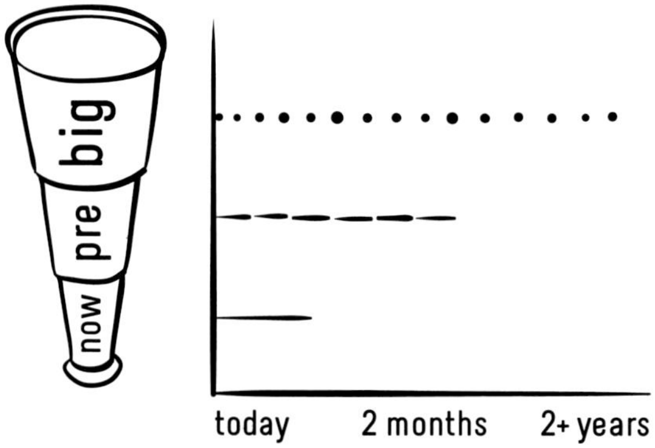

3 Views on a Timeline

You don't necessarily start with the Big-View. Instead, you might define scope at a high level and then define product options for the Pre-View (your first release). From there, you might dive into the Now-View (your first iteration or release). This "jump right in" approach may help the team develop a rhythm of continual delivery.

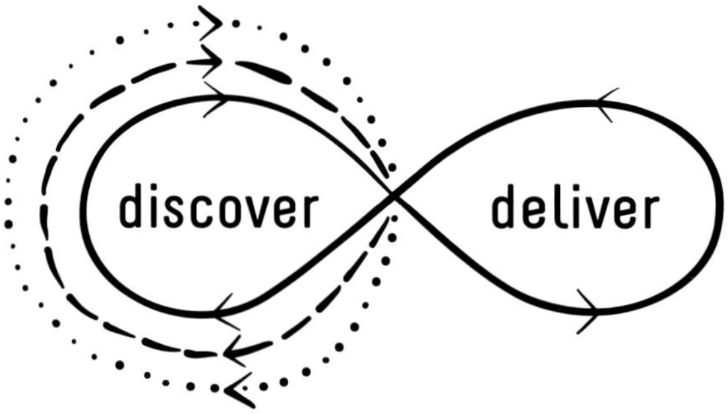

Wants: generalized, high-level product options wanted to realize the product vision over time.

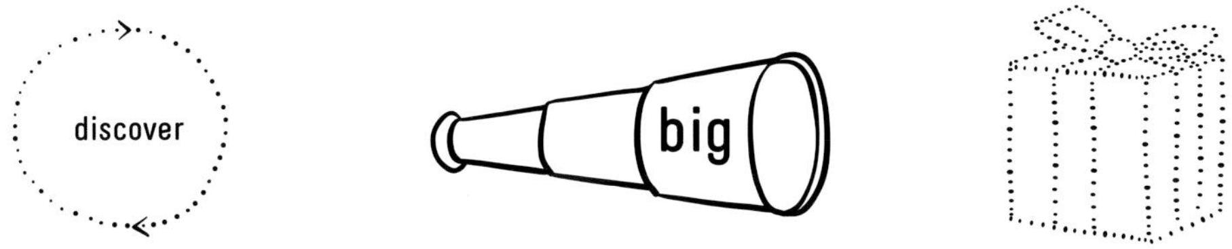

Needs: product options needed for the next release.

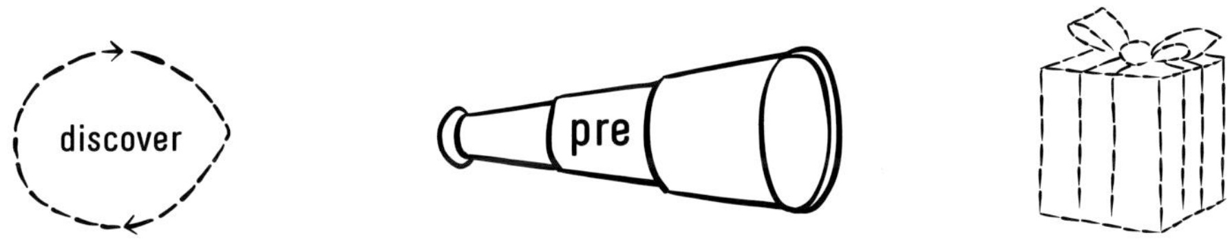

Requirements: product options required, with sufficient detail to develop.

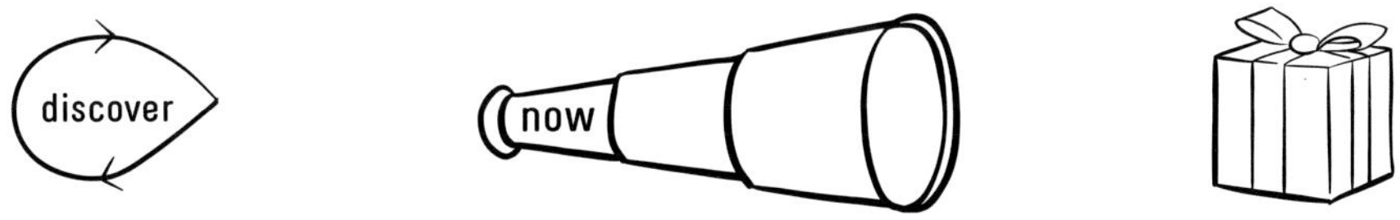

Product Options: Wanted, Needed, Required

Plans by Views

Plan Name	View	Plan's Purpose	Participating Partners
Product roadmap, portfolio roadmap	Big-View	Identify delivery cycles for product's highest-value options	• Sponsor, product champion • Business executives representing product management, marketing, sales, strategy, lines of business • Strategic technology advisers
Release plan, product queue	Pre-View	Identify the product's highest-value options to deliver in the next release	• Strategic and tactical product champions • Entire delivery team • Technology advisers
Iteration or sprint plan (for timebox delivery); Product queue (for low delivery)	Now-View	Identify highest-value options to deliver in current delivery cycle	• Tactical product champion • Entire delivery team

Roadmaps

The Big-View plan—the one that outlines how the product will evolve over time to realize the product vision—is typically called a product roadmap.

Various kinds of product roadmaps communicate different things to different audiences. *Commercial products* often have internal and *external roadmaps*. An *internal roadmap* is used to communicate with internal stakeholders. An external roadmap, a subset of the internal roadmap, reveals your product vision and features; engages customers, investors, and external partners; promotes market innovation; or shakes up the marketplace. It excludes candidate solutions you don't want to share externally for a number of reasons (e.g., to maintain flexibility, to delay commitment, to allow time for determining feasibility, to retain strategic or competitive advantage). Cadences for roadmaps vary. A time-based roadmap shows which product options will be delivered at regular releases, key milestones, industry occurrences, or market events. Other roadmaps are based on business readiness, regulatory compliance, or market needs.

The Impact of Risks and Dependencies on the Plan

Risks and dependencies, both internal and external, constrain the plan. You may choose to avoid risks or consider ways to mitigate their impact on the plan. Dependencies include people (e.g., teams or organizations), other systems, suppliers, infrastructure (networks, devices), and organizational readiness. There may be risks related to the product (delivering the wrong product, at the wrong time, to the wrong market), technology, and the team (not being co-located, being unfamiliar with the product domain, having an unavailable product champion). You account for dependencies and risks so that you can deliver candidate solutions in the optimum sequence, minimize rework, and maximize business, customer, and technical value.

Plan Essentials

Collaborative: Plans are based on collaborative decision making by the product partners. You balance your understanding of the product options with a hard-nosed assessment of which are most valuable for the next planning horizon.

Flexible: You need the flexibility to adjust the product plans at any time based on what you've learned from stakeholder feedback, new information, and market conditions. Post-delivery, you continually validate released solutions to learn how to adapt the product or possibly even terminate it.

Ongoing: The product evolves as enhancements and extensions are added until it is retired, replaced, or withdrawn. If you achieve sufficient value sooner than expected or if you're not gaining the expected value, it may be best to end development.

Appropriately defined: A plan includes a theme (which might include the customer segment being served), candidate solutions and their acceptance criteria, preconditions (e.g., committed sponsor, funding, people to implement the plan, technologies in place), and risk mitigation actions.

The acceptance criteria serve as essential ingredients for negotiating and allocating the optimal product options. You also decide when you will validate that the anticipated outcomes (objectives) match the actual results.

Structured Conversation

The partners use structured conversations to discover product needs by continually exploring and evaluating product options, crafting candidate solutions, and confirming that they will meet business objectives.

The structured conversation is a metaphor for the ongoing, systematic, and collaborative discovery and delivery of product options. It's a creative process that supports the product partners as they holistically and iteratively learn about product options.

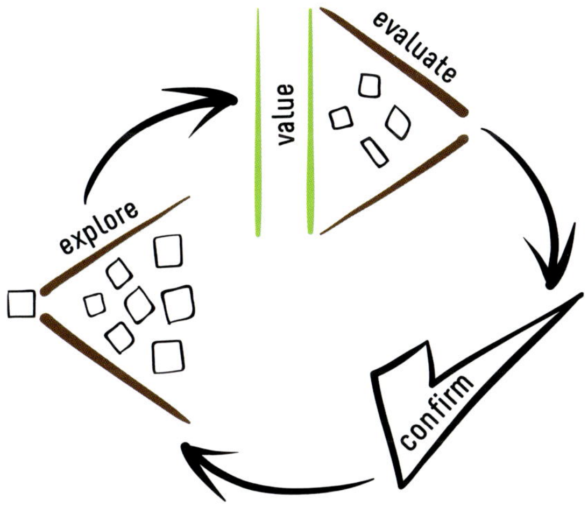

The Structured Conversation

How do you collaborate to build a shared, holistic understanding of product options? How do you decide what to deliver? How do you allocate candidate solutions to different delivery cycles? How do you verify that you're building the right product—before it's delivered? How do you validate that you've built the right solution after delivery?

The structured conversation is a lightweight framework that guides the partners as they learn about the product's possibilities and decide what to deliver.

Shared Learning

The 7 Product Dimensions support a holistic and integrated way to learn about the product. The partners explore each of the 7 Product Dimensions of a product option, evaluate each option to identify the most valuable and cohesive candidate solutions for the next planning horizon, and confirm that the selected candidate solutions meet the intended goals.

The structured conversation is used in any planning view for continual collaboration.

A key benefit of this iterative approach is that the technology partners learn more about business imperatives, and the product champion and other business experts learn more about the technical aspects of the evolving product. As your team members question, challenge, and clarify the filtering criteria, you all deepen your understanding of the business domain and the options that will provide value. This continual learning improves your ability to estimate, uncover, and manage uncertainties and risks and to raise questions for further discovery.

Advantages

The structured conversation is usable in all problem domains, leverages the discipline of analysis, is quick to learn and efficient to use, engages all product partners, and deepens their knowledge of product options. The structured conversation helps you to optimize value, minimize delays, mitigate risks, and clarify shared expectations.

You converse with the end in mind—using acceptance criteria as tangible measures to explore and evaluate product options and validate your hypothesis about the value of the candidate solution. Whether you're enhancing a mature product or creating a new and innovative one, you can use the structured conversation. The timeframe for discovery and delivery tends to be very short (e.g., daily or even hourly) for innovative products, and longer (e.g., weekly, monthly, quarterly) for mature products.

The ongoing structured conversation may be called discovery, pruning, preparing, optioning, or refining product options. The conversation's cadence varies depending on the team's *delivery method—timebox or flow.*

Teams taking a timebox approach have weekly or biweekly planning sessions. Teams using flow (*Kanban*) may replenish the *input queue* when a slot opens or after a review. This might be referred to as *upstream* discovery or queue replenishment.

Explore, Evaluate, Confirm

The structured conversation is a creative and disciplined way to build shared understanding and make decisions. It involves three key activities: explore, evaluate, and confirm.

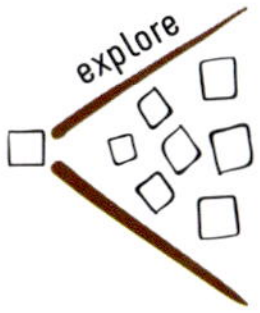

You explore options for the 7 Product Dimensions, using the product vision, goals, and objectives as your guide. You use expansive thinking to uncover multiple options or possibilities.

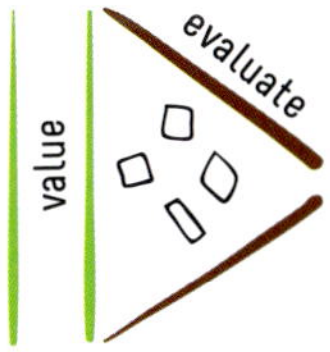

Using the business goals, objectives, and value considerations as your filter, you evaluate each option's benefits, risks, and dependencies. You make decisions and identify the high-value candidate solutions. Then you allocate each candidate solution to a delivery cycle.

You define acceptance criteria to verify and validate each candidate solution.

Explore, Evaluate, Confirm Product Options

Conversing Across Views

You converse continually across the three planning views. As the planning horizon gets closer, you move the product options from possibilities (wants) to probabilities (needs) to actualities (requirements). This successive elaboration incorporates diverse stakeholder perspectives, transparent decision making, systematic thinking, and deep learning.

Discovery may start at any view and move to any other view. You might begin in the Now-View or Pre-View and find that you need to move back up to the Big-View—and vice versa. Wherever you begin, you draw on scenarios and tangible examples to help you explore product options.

Enriching the Conversation

As you conduct your structured conversation, you can use a variety of tools to creatively engage the partners to quickly explore and evaluate product options. As in all conversations, the partners talk, listen, and use analytical thinking, which thrives on logic, reduction, and ranking. You might aid the conversation by using examples to make the options concrete.

A robust structured conversation employs visualization. You use analysis models to draw relationships and dependencies and depict product options using analysis models. You might employ high-tech tools as well as low-tech media such as whiteboards, walls, and charts. Your visuals might be temporary, or they might be repurposed for documenting, building, and packaging the product (see Section 6, Tools & Techniques).

Section 3

THE 7 PRODUCT DIMENSIONS

THE 7 PRODUCT DIMENSIONS

The 7 Product Dimensions represent categories of the product.

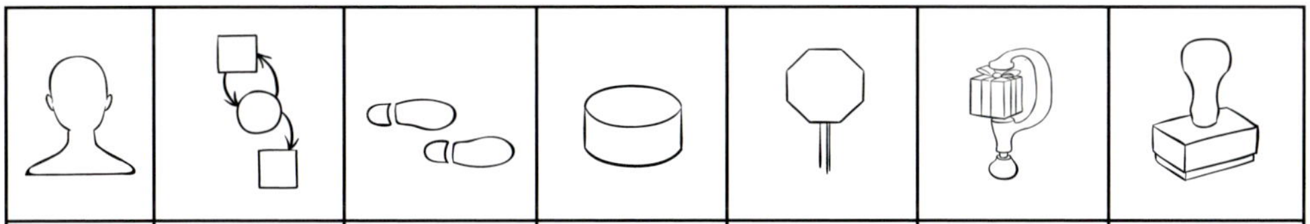

User	Interface	Action	Data	Control	Environment	Quality Attribute
Users interact with the product	The product connects to users, systems, and devices	The product provides capabilities for users	The product includes a repository of data and useful information	The product enforces constraints	The product conforms to physical properties and technology platforms	The product has certain properties that qualify its operation and development

The 7 Product Dimensions are used at all three planning views: the Big-View, the Pre-View, and the Now-View.

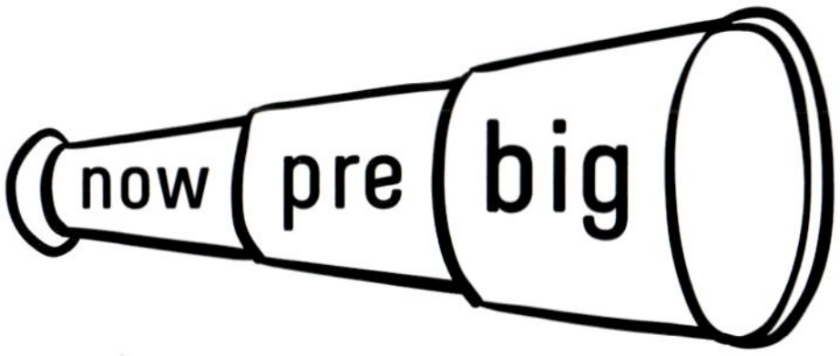

The Planning Views

You can start your structured conversation with any one dimension and then navigate to other dimensions.

Comprehensive, holistic understanding of product needs

The beauty of the 7 Product Dimensions is that they guide you toward a comprehensive understanding of the product. In other words, conversing holistically across the 7 Product Dimensions helps you to discover product possibilities and plan your deliveries.

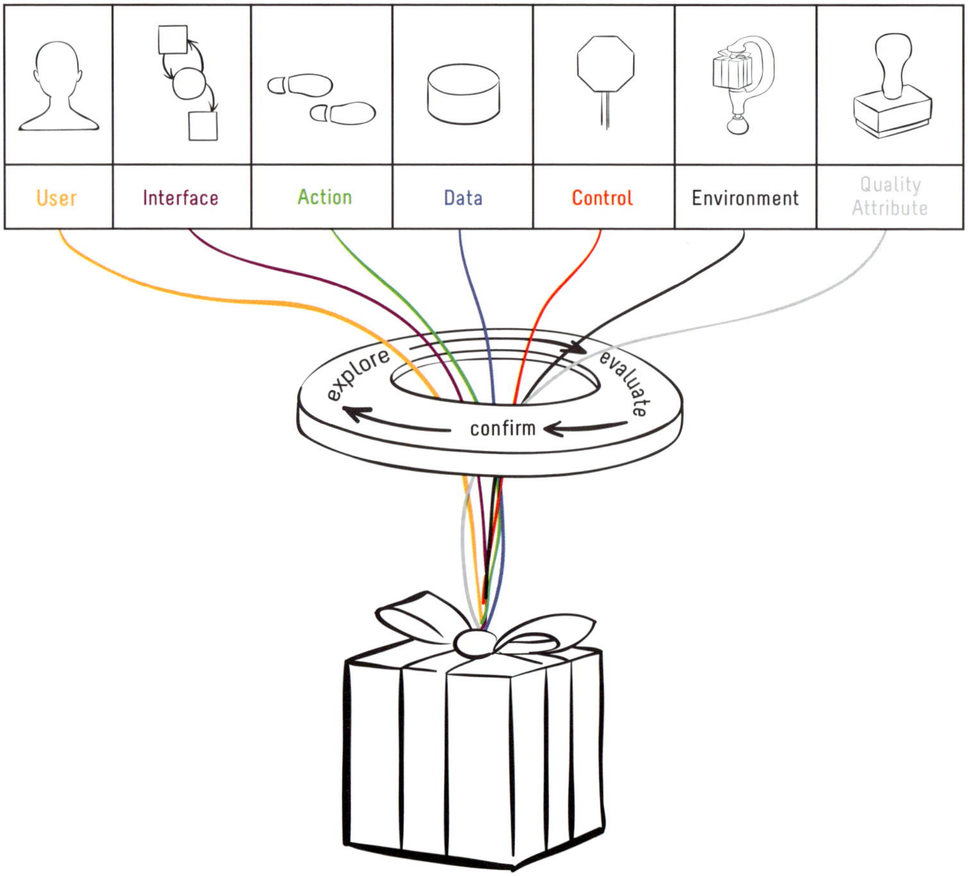

Holistic, Comprehensive Product

Interrelated Dimensions

A product dimension focuses on one aspect of the product, yet does not stand alone. Each dimension relates to and is dependent on other dimensions. The 7 Product Dimensions canvas illustrates the relationships among the dimensions.

The 7 Product Dimension Canvas

The position of each dimension on the canvas reflects the dimensions' relationships. Here are some examples:

A user interacts with the product through interfaces.
An action operates on data.
A control may constrain data.
An action must be available (quality attribute) during specific times.
An interface must operate in an environment.

When you explore and evaluate one dimension, it leads the conversation to other dimensions, exposing missing, inconsistent, or erroneous product dimensions.

Representing the 7 Product Dimensions

You can use a variety of ways to express your product's dimensions, including visual models and text descriptions. It's a good idea to select the minimum combination you need to reach a shared understanding of the product.

User

Users interact with the product.

Who values the product?
Who benefits from it?
Who uses it?

A product exists to serve its users. A user may be a person, another product, or a system that interacts with your product. A user may play many roles as they engage with the product. You explore and analyze the users to learn their roles and goals.

User Examples

Persona	Charlie, a junior customer service rep
User Role	Service Scheduler

Leading with User

Consider starting your structured conversation with the User Dimension when you have customers with high-volume transactions; customers with high-revenue usage; new customers in a new market; add a new customer segment in an existing market.

Squeeky Kleen's sales manager has been thinking about partnering with real estate agents. The agents could recommend SK's services to home sellers: "It would be a good idea to get your windows cleaned before the open house. Here's a coupon from Squeeky Kleen." The team explores the related Action options (capture referral, reward agents for referrals, etc.), Data options (reward amount, coupon identifier), and Control options (coupon expiration rules). There also may be nonfunctional product dimensions to consider, such as Interface options for distributing coupons.

Ways to Represent the User Dimension

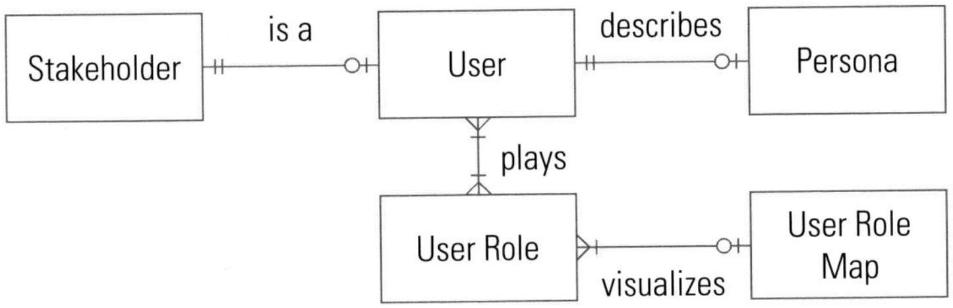

Interface

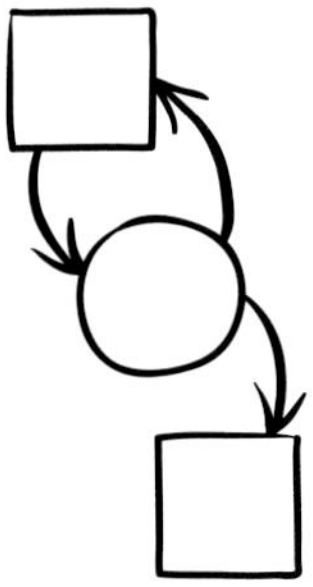

A product connects to users, systems, and devices.

What interfaces do you need to build for the users to interact with the product?
How does the product receive data?
How does the product send data?

An interface is the mechanism that users or other systems employ to exchange data with the product. You may choose to prototype new or changing interfaces as a means to discover and analyze product options.

Interface Examples

User interface	Customer provides service request details. Customer receives a confirmation. Customer service rep calls a customer to follow up on a completed job.
Hardware device interface	Cleaner's handheld device sends the customer's job completion signature to SK.
System-to-system interface	SK's Inventory system sends an order to the Wholesale Distributor.

Leading with Interface

Consider starting your structured conversation with the Interface Dimension when you need to create a packaged solution with multiple interfaces to internal and external systems or integrate multiple external parties, both human and software.

The SK product champion wants to explore a new interface: using text messaging to remind a customer of an upcoming job. The team asks which customers (User) will receive the message, what will trigger the Action to send the message, what the Data will be (content of the message, number to which to send the message), which Controls apply (any rules and calculations), which Quality Attributes apply (security, performance), and the Environments to be used (devices that will be supported).

Ways to Represent the Interface Dimension

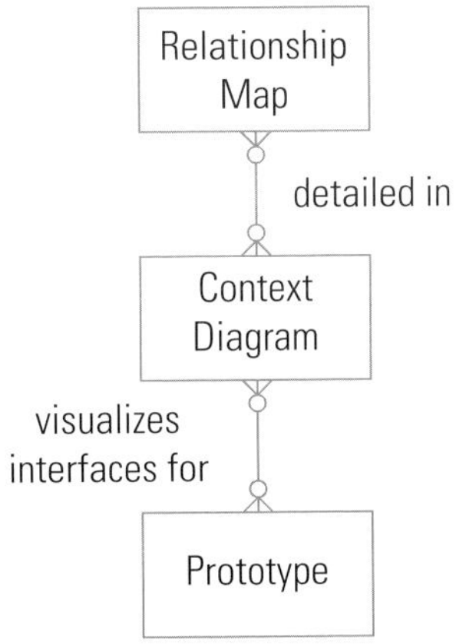

Action

The product provides capabilities for users.

How do actions provide business value?
How is an action triggered?
How does the product respond?
How are actions sequenced?
How do actions impact data?

The Actions Dimension of a product represents activities that achieve results that the users need. An event triggers an action to execute the product's planned responses (which are also actions). The event may be initiated by users, by a predefined time, or by a predecessor action. An action may enforce controls (e.g., policies, rules). Actions transform data into usable information for users.

You elaborate and decompose high-value actions to an atomic level that enables you to unambiguously develop and test the action. You allocate actions that will be automated to a software solution. Non-automated actions must be integrated with the software and supported by it.

Action Examples

Event	Customer contacts SK to arrange for a service.
Business Process	Schedule a Job
User Story	As a customer, I need to schedule services at a time that is convenient for me so that...
Scenario	Roger Smith needs to schedule window cleaning services at his residential property on Saturday morning.

Leading with Action

Consider starting your structured conversation with the Actions Dimension when your domain is: accounting; administration; billing; business operations; demand management; event-controlled real-time processing; human resources; inventory management; materials management; loan management; logistics; operations; order processing; payroll; or process automation workflow.

The Squeeky Kleen CEO dreams up new functionality: a "Bright Day" cleaning program, where customers earn points that they can redeem for future discounts. The team uses the Action Dimension to explore options for registering, tracking, and redeeming the points. They explore which customers (User) qualify, they identify the Data and Control options, and they define options for the nonfunctional product dimensions.

Ways to Represent the Action Dimension

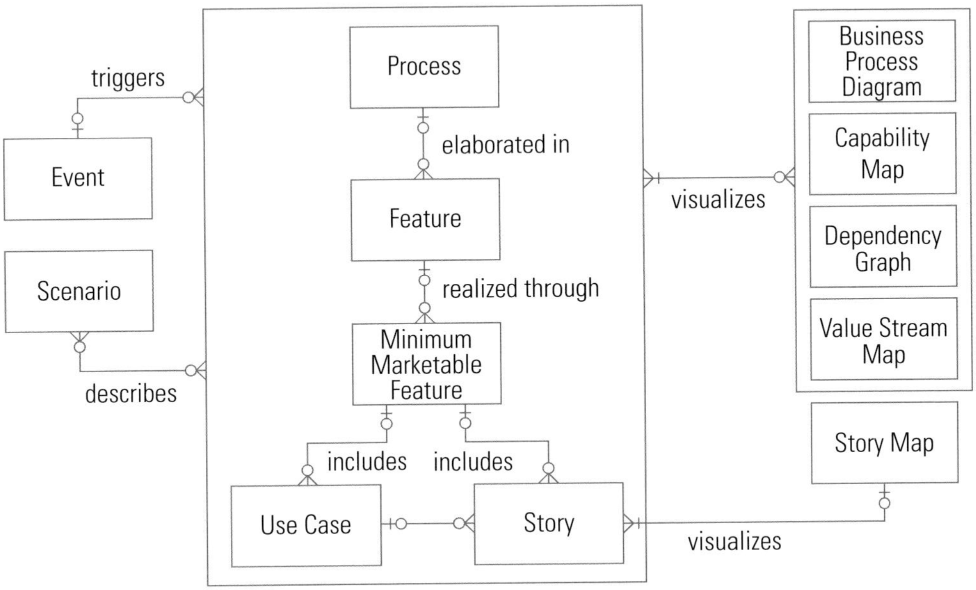

Data

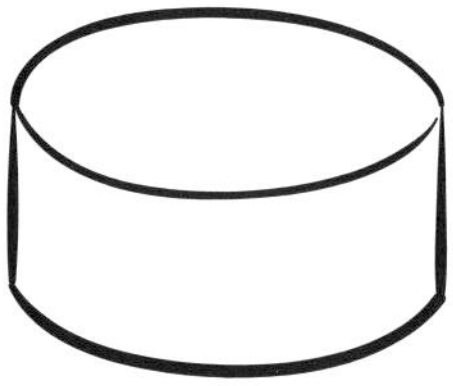

A product includes a repository of data and useful information.

What data do users need from the product?
What data does the product receive? From where?
What data must the product store? How do you know whether the data is valid?
For how long is the data valid? What is the context in which the data has meaning?

The Data Dimension of a product represents data (raw facts) and information (interpreted data) needed to support the product's users. Data and information are essential for making business decisions. Actions transform data into a useful context for users. The sources of data include external systems and users.

You elaborate and decompose high-value data into elementary *data attributes*. For data that must be represented and accounted for in the software, you use data models showing all product data at rest, organized into groupings and relationships. As the product grows in functionality, the data to be stored also expands.

Data Examples

Data Domain	Financial
Data Entity	Payment
Data Attribute	Payment amount

Leading with Data

Consider starting your structured conversation with the Data Dimension when your domain is business intelligence; customer relationship management; or data warehousing, analysis, querying, and reporting.

Squeeky Kleen's operations manager requests statistics on the cleaners' activities so she can evaluate the effectiveness of the scheduling. She is looking for a variety of data: the number of jobs completed per cleaner, per day/week/month; the amount of time spent traveling to and from jobs; lost time due to customers not calling to cancel within the cancellation period, and so on. The team needs to explore what event will trigger the Action to produce the report, any Controls (rules and calculations) used to summarize the data, the related Quality Attributes (security, usability), and the Environment (devices that present the report to the user).

Ways to Represent the Data Dimension

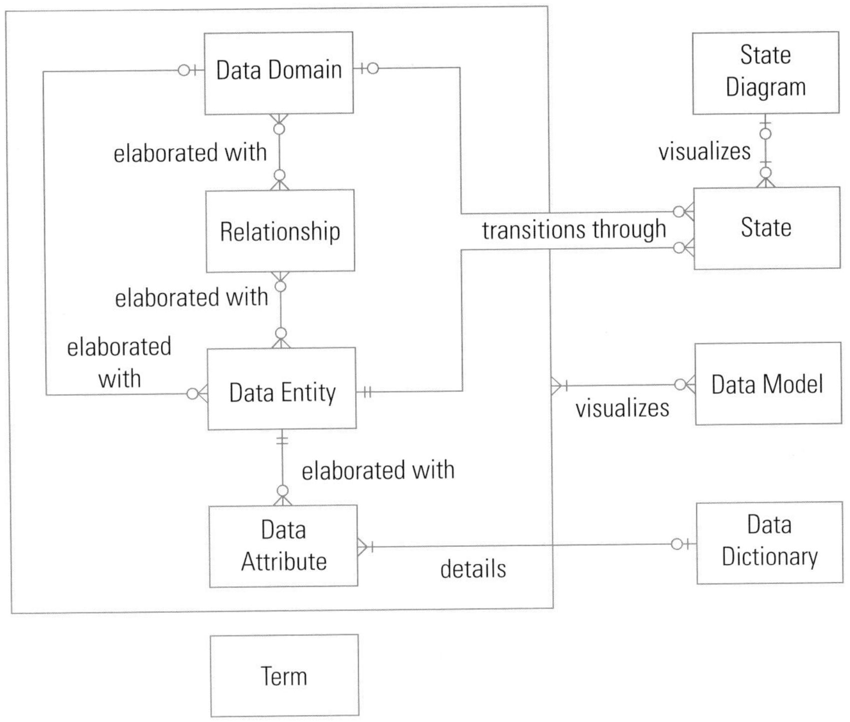

Control

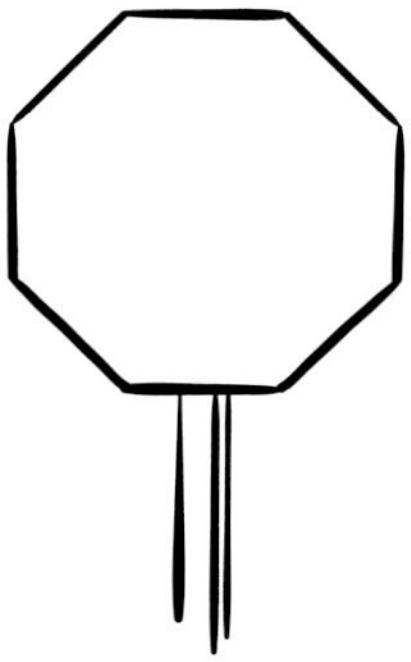

A product enforces constraints.

Why are you motivated to conform to policies and regulations?
What are the risks if you do not comply with control needs?
What violations must be detected?
What is the jurisdiction of a given policy, regulation, or rule?
What is the enforcement level for the rule?

The Control Dimension of a product represents guidelines or constraints on the conduct of the business. They provide a basis for decision making. A system must be able to evaluate such controls and use them to direct appropriate action. Whether the controls originate from the business itself or from external sources (e.g., regulatory agencies), you must articulate controls in a manner that can be validated. Typically, you express controls as clearly defined statements or acceptance tests.

Controls exist regardless of their enforcement mechanism—whether they are enforced in software, manually through a business process, or both. When necessary for compliance, controls must be traceable from code back to the originating source.

You can organize complex controls in *decision tables* or *decision trees*. The team determines whether a control will be enforced via software or manually as part of human work, depending on value, risks, and dependencies.

Control Examples

Business Policy	A customer who has not paid for prior services may be prevented from scheduling new services.
Business Rule	An individual customer whose total delinquent payment amount is greater than $250 must not schedule new services.

Leading with Control

Consider starting your structured conversation with the Control Dimension when your domain is about clinical diagnosis; claim adjudication; credit checking; financial risk analysis; fraud detection; loan underwriting; power and network usage; product configuration or regulatory imperatives.

Squeeky Kleen learns about a new or revised regulation that must be addressed soon—or else the company will be in violation of the law and incur fines, suffer public embarrassment, or even shut down. The team explores any Action options needed to enforce the Controls, any related Data, and any Interface needs, as well as Quality Attribute and Environment options.

What's the difference between controls and actions?

An action is a predefined business behavior. An action may enforce a control.

Examples: Compare canceled date and time with SK's cancellation terms.

Assess any cancellation fee.

A control (policy or *business rule)* states what must be true.

A control guides or constrains an action.

Policy example: A cancellation may be assessed a cancellation fee.

Business Rule example: A Job canceled less than 1 business day prior to the Job's scheduled date must be charged a cancellation fee.

Why separate controls from actions?

Knowing the difference lets you clearly evaluate the options for each dimension. It lets the business quickly adapt to continuous changes in its controls. Actions seldom change as often as controls.

Ways to Represent the Contol Dimension

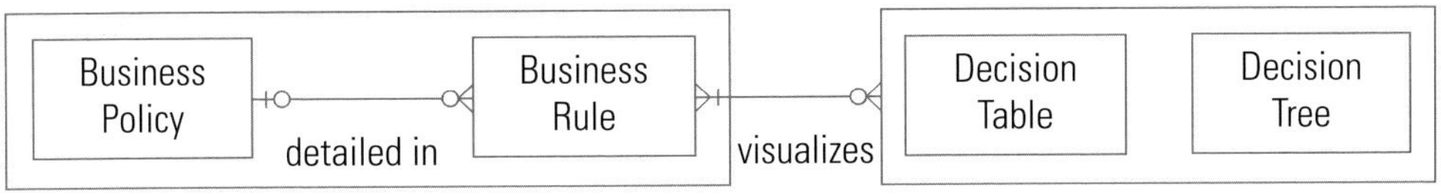

Environment

A product conforms to physical properties and technology platforms.

Where will the product be used? From what physical locations?
What are the product's physical properties?
What technologies and physical means will be used to install, configure, access, revise, license, protect, adapt, or dispose of the product?
Does the product need to conform to certain technology standards?
How do development and operational environment options affect quality attributes?

The Environment Dimension of the product includes the operational and development environment.

The *operational environment* includes the in-use product's physical properties and its technology platform. The operational environment is specific to a location and possibly to specific users and product actions. This environment has physical properties that need to be understood, such as the place and space where the product will be operated, the product's external and internal composition, and mechanisms for accessing the product.

The *development environment* governs how the product will be architected, developed, tested, deployed, and released into service. The development environment is composed of the hardware, software, and standards that make up its technology platform.

Both the operational and the development environments use a *technology platform*. The technology platform includes hardware components, software components, and the standards used to develop and operate the product. Technology platform hardware includes physical equipment, media, and devices that contain software. Technology platform software is the set of components that manage the plumbing underlying the product. Standards provide common protocols for software and hardware development, deployment, and operation.

Operational Environment Examples

User	Location Physical	Properties
CSR	SK office	Noisy, congested office space

Development Environment Examples

Software	Hardware	Standards
GreatBrowser3.2	Cassidy3500Router	DistributedDataStandard 4.3

Leading with Environment

Consider starting your structured conversation with the Environment Dimension when you need to add or change technology platforms or physical locations for an existing application.

Due to low cash flow, SK management wants to launch an "immediate pay" capability. This will permit the cleaner to collect payment from a customer on-site, after completing the work. The team starts the conversation by exploring the physical Environment options (the location where a payment will take place) as well as hardware options (the Interfaces dimension) for capturing the customer's payment details and signature and the physical properties of a payment device. The conversation extends to options for Actions (verify the payment method), Data (payment method, credit card details), and Quality Attributes (security and response time).

Ways to Represent the Environment Dimension

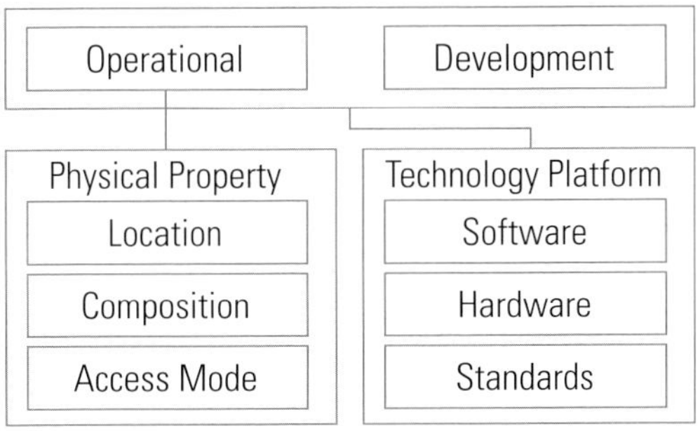

Quality Attribute

A product has certain properties that qualify its operation and development.

How will you know whether the quality attributes satisfy the partners' needs?
How will you test and measure the quality attributes?
Do quality attributes apply to all or only a subset of the product options?
Can the quality attributes be implemented incrementally?
What degree of specificity do you need?

The quality attributes are predefined levels of service for the product's functionality and interfaces. Quality attributes describe operation and development properties for the product's User, Interface, Action, and Data dimensions. For example, a user story might be qualified by multiple quality attributes, such as performance, security, and usability. A quality attribute might be specific to one or more users, interfaces, actions, or data entities. Some quality attributes—for example, audit, authentication, localization, *reliability*, and *security*—may apply to more than one dimension.

Quality Attribute Examples

Availability	The SK scheduling application will be available 95% of the time Monday through Friday from 8:00 a.m. to 5:00 p.m. Eastern. The SK scheduling application will be available 95% of the time on Saturday from 8:00 a.m. to 2 p.m. Eastern.
Installability	An untrained user will be able to install upgrades to the SK application within 10 minutes without accessing any printed documentation.

Leading with Quality Attribute

Consider starting your structured conversation with the Quality Attribute Dimension when you need to enable new or changing *availability*, performance, *portability*, scalability, security; or increase development efficiencies.

SK's business is growing so quickly that it needs to expand its hours. Management decides to be open Monday through Friday from 8 a.m. to 7 p.m. and Saturday from 7 a.m. to 4 p.m. Eastern time. The team starts the conversation by exploring Quality Attributes (system availability) and then considers which Users (CSRs and cleaners) need to access which Actions (estimating, scheduling, and payment) using which operational Environments (working virtually or in the SK office).

What is the difference between actions, controls, and quality attributes?

An action is a business behavior that creates, reads, updates, or deletes business domain data.

Example: Schedule a residential cleaning job.

A control (a business policy or business rule) guides business judgments and decisions, regardless of the implementation environment.

Example: A requested location (postal code) must be within an area supported by SK on the requested service date.

A quality attribute is neither an action nor a control. Rather, a quality attribute defines a quantifiable property the system must exhibit.

Example (performance): The calculated price for requested services must be displayed within 2 seconds of entering the service type and count.

Quality attributes: Neglected, forgotten, or delayed

A product's Quality Attribute Dimension is sometimes neglected, forgotten, or delayed. Conversations about product options tend to focus more on functional dimensions such as Users, Actions, Data, and Controls. Some product teams struggle to converse about quality attributes with customer and business partners, because of the technical nature of the topic. Other teams struggle with identifying the possible and achievable levels of quality attributes without testing or experimenting with them.

Yet it is often essential to satisfy quality attribute service levels if you are to achieve business value. If you don't deliver acceptable quality attribute levels early on (performance, security, usability, and so on), your product's success may be threatened.

Transparently discuss the balance between the cost of delay (the "opportunity cost") for deferring implementation of high-value quality attributes against the cost of rework and additional testing you may incur to implement those quality attributes later.

Ways to Represent the Quality Attribute Dimension

Operational

- Availability
- Recoverability
- Installability
- Robustness
- Interoperability
- Safety
- Performance
- Scalability
- Reliability
- Security
- Usability

Development

- Efficency
- Flexibility
- Modifiability
- Portability
- Reusability
- Testibilty

Adapted from: Gottesdiener, 2005

Section 4

THE STRUCTURED CONVERSATION

THE STRUCTURED CONVERSATION

Explore, Evaluate, Confirm

The structured conversation is a discussion framework for collaboration. It is ongoing, generative, and based on continual learning.

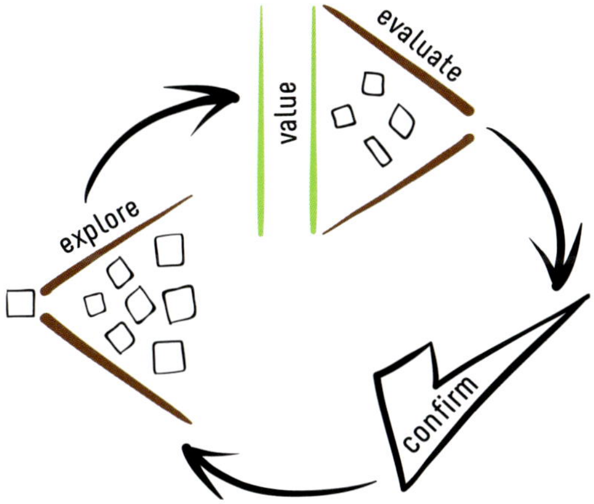

The Structured Conversation

Explore product needs to discover options across all product dimensions.

You explore product needs frequently and continually. Exploration may take the form of spontaneous, just-in-time conversations that take place as technology partners are about to implement product options. You also explore product needs at scheduled intervals as you plan deliveries.

Evaluate options using value considerations.

You assess the benefits and risks of options. You consider product dependencies in making value decisions, as you assemble high-value options into candidate solutions. You then allocate candidate solutions to planning horizons.

Confirm that the product is fit for use and accomplishes its business objectives.

You identify acceptance criteria for the candidate solution. You also specify measures to assess whether the delivered solution accomplishes its intended ends. Your goal is to learn how additional deliveries can be adjusted to optimize business value.

On an on-going basis, you use retrospectives to continually improve your structured conversations.

The structured conversation is used in all planning views:
Big-View, Pre-View, and Now-View.

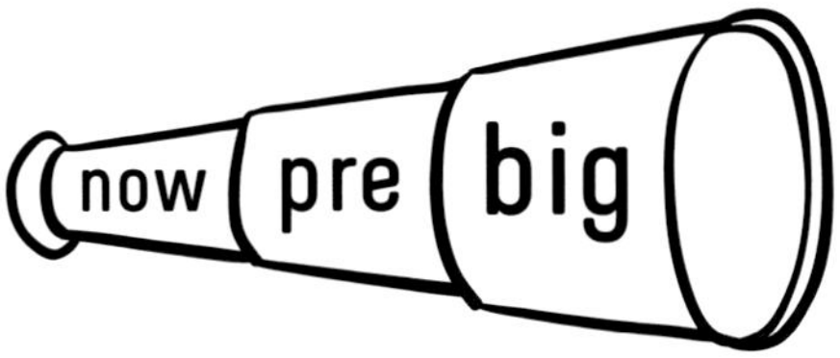

The Planning Views

Explore

You search for product options.

What options might help you achieve your product's goals?
How do you holistically reveal product options?

Explore to Learn

Exploration is an iterative process of imagining product possibilities. Some people refer to it as ideation, envisioning, or innovating. During exploration, the partners collaborate to expose product options that will deliver value.

As you explore product possibilities, you are continually learning. You analyze the competition, examine existing and potential markets and customers, and study technology trends and capabilities. You dig into the organization's expectations for the product and assess the technical possibilities. You also incorporate feedback from prior deliveries.

Exploration takes many forms: researching, questioning, inquiring, and inventing product options. In all cases, you strive to stay open to possibilities and remain nonjudgmental.

Exploring the 7 Product Dimensions

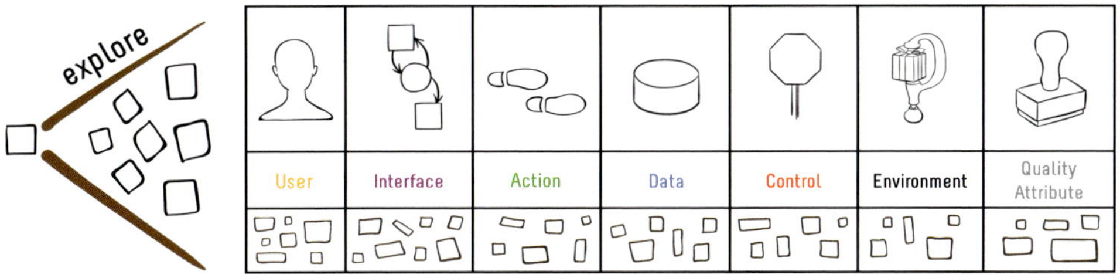

Exploring Options for the 7 Product Dimensions

Exploration thrives on an open, inquiring mind-set. The input to this exploration is the product's vision, goals, and objectives.

One approach is to write a narrative of a user's *journey* (a large scenario) in using the product. This narrative often focuses on a few dimensions: the actions and possibly the interfaces. Note that it is vital to explore all 7 Product Dimensions to gain a holistic understanding of the product options.

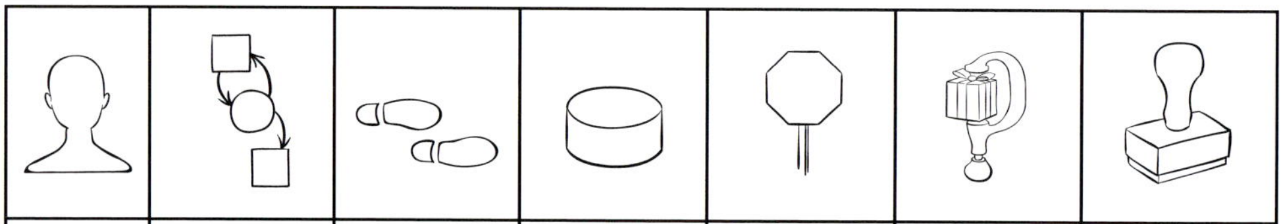

User	Interface	Action	Data	Control	Environment	Quality Attribute
What users could this product serve?	What interfaces are possible?	What actions are possible?	What data could be acted on?	What controls might need to be enforced?	What are the product's possible operational and development environments?	What quality attributes could constrain and control the product?

Sample Explore Questions

Patterns That Work

- Engage your business, user, and technology partners early and often as you conduct structured conversations.
- Stay focused on the current planning horizon (Big-View, Pre-View, Now-View).
- Use the *Scenario Z Pattern*, scenarios, examples, and *user acceptance tests* to explore and verify the options.
- Keep it light. Don't dive down into details beyond your current view.
- Let it be low-fidelity. Allow your representations to be partial and incomplete, rather than finished and detailed, renderings of that dimension. Hand-drawn, unfinished analysis models are often good enough to test for shared understanding.

Resources for Exploring

Effective exploration is focused on uncovering ways to achieve the product's vision, goals, and objectives by learning what the partners need or want. A number of techniques are available. Here's a partial list:

- Contextual inquiry (studying users in their work or play space)
- Service design (a set of innovative thinking tools that draws on user-centered design)
- Observation and job shadowing
- Exploratory prototypes
- Interviews
- *Facilitated workshops* using expansive thinking techniques such as brainstorming, mindmaps, brainwriting, innovation games, and role-playing
- Research-based techniques such as:
    - Industry research (in a vertical business, market, or customer segment)
    - Surveys, focus groups, customer complaints and suggestions
    - Competitive analysis (using or reverse engineering a competitor product)
    - Existing documentation (if it's reliable)

Exploring the User Experience

Understanding users is vital when you're building software products. Often, the success or failure of a product can be traced to the user interface. User experience is the overarching term for topics that include studying users' *mental models* to arrive at a useful and usable product design.

As you decide to what degree and in which way to explore the user experience, you consider the number of users, their accessibility and environment, how much time you have to conduct the exploration, and the quality of the feedback you hope to receive.

Evaluate

You decide on the candidate solutions for delivery.

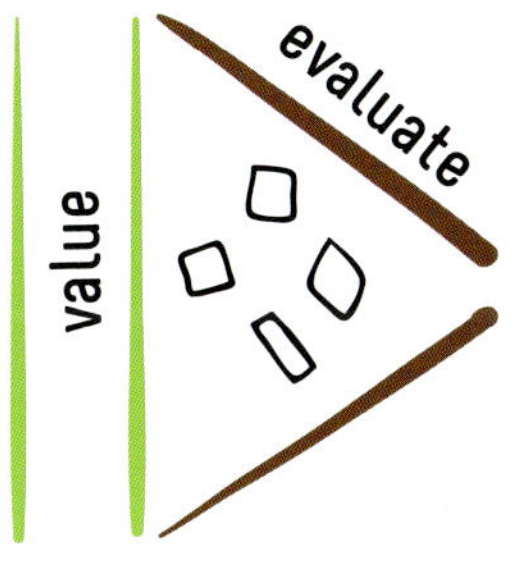

Which product options will optimize value?
How do you reach a shared commitment on candidate solutions to deliver next?
How do dependencies and risks affect your evaluation decisions?
What is the optimum sequence for delivery?

Evaluate to Learn

Your goal is to obtain business value as soon as possible. In this way you can gain market share, address the needs of various *market segments,* enable earlier releases to fund subsequent releases, protect revenue, and shield your reputation against regulatory violations.

Evaluating the 7 Product Dimensions

You can evaluate the 7 Product Dimensions in any order.

You evaluate each option, balancing benefits, risks, and dependences, and identify the high-value options.

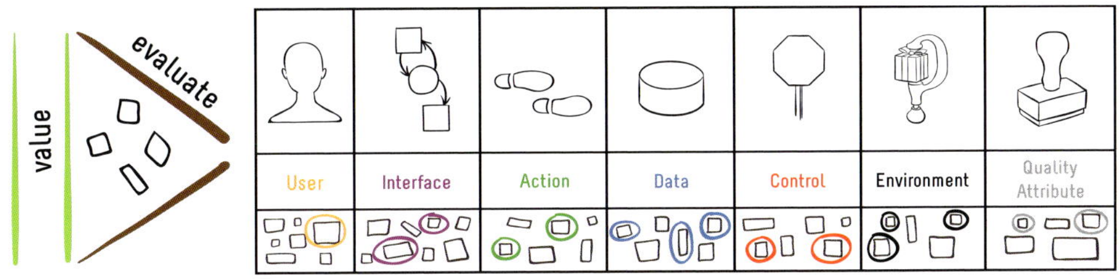

Evaluating each of the 7 Product Dimensions Options

User	Interface	Action	Data	Control	Environment	Quality Attribute
Which user options interact most frequently with the product?	Which interface options will provide a valuable user experience?	Which action options are date or time sensitive?	Which data options are needed to support the high-valued action options?	Which control options must be strictly enforced to avoid compliance fines?	Which operational and development environment options will affect organizational readiness?	Which quality attribute options will the partners find more crucial?

Sample Evaluate Questions

Evaluating Across the 7 Product Dimensions

To define a candidate solution, you identify cohesive combinations of high-value options.

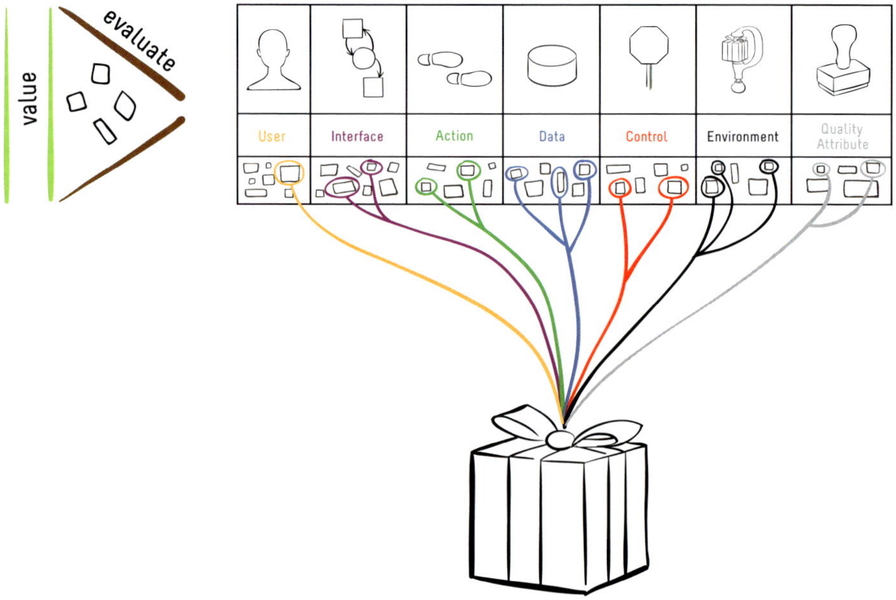

Evaluating across the 7 Product Dimensions – A Candidate Solution

You consider the collective value of the high-value options. You can adjust (raise or lower) the value of a specific option due to benefits, risks, and dependencies. You can also uncover missing, erroneous, or conflicting options. The goal is to assemble viable combinations of options that together deliver cohesive functionality and usability to the customer—a successful candidate solution.

Here are sample evaluation questions for assembling options:

- Which option combinations will be easier or least costly to test?
- Which will have higher delivery risk due to new or untested technology?
- What trade-offs among options might pose technical risks?
- Which options will be easier or least costly to test? Which options have flexibility, providing greater technical value during delivery?

Evaluating Candidate Solutions

To identify candidate solutions for delivery, you evaluate options within and across the 7 Product Dimensions. You assess each product option's relative value (using the partners' value considerations) to make value decisions. You compare options and combinations of options to arrive at a candidate solution. You consider benefits, risks, and dependencies to identify the highest-value candidate solutions for any given timeframe.

As you consider the possibilities, you keep an eye on the product's vision, goals, and objectives. You use the most current understanding of value, while remaining open to adjusting that value due to internal and external changes.

value

As you evaluate product options, you continue to learn about the product and expand your understanding of the partners' value considerations. You reorder options as needed to agree on the most valuable options to include in the candidate solution.

You may also need to resolve differing, competing, or conflicting perspectives to reach decisions. You support the decision-making process by using collaborative, participatory methods to reach closure. Not only do such methods speed the work, but they also help to ensure that all voices are heard. You might use themes (or *motifs*) to structure your evaluation conversations. Your theme might target a particular customer or market, a new or improved product *capability*, or a regulatory issue. Themes can also relate to *strategies* (actions you take to realize business goals).

Size Matters

A key step in identifying a candidate solution is to estimate how big it is and how long it will take to build, based on the complexity of the work and the known *velocity* or *cycle time*. A candidate solution may be a small, implementable item (an *MMF* or *MVP)*. You may group candidate solutions for delivery. The size of a candidate solution may depend on the life cycle of the product, customer readiness, and business needs.

> ### Keeping Your Backlog Lean
> To maintain a lean, healthy backlog and to minimize cycle time, store only the selected options in your product backlog or queue. Leftover product options—those not selected for the candidate solution—may be discarded. Some teams choose to record them or photograph walls that show them listed, along with the rationale for not choosing them. You may find this practice helpful if team turnover is high or you're working in a regulatory environment.

Planning: Allocate Candidate Solutions

As you identify and evaluate your candidate solutions, you allocate them to a plan. It's best to use collaborative decision making, incorporating the collective knowledge, skills, and experience of all the partners. By resolving their divergent perspectives, you can arrive at the best possible decision at a given time.

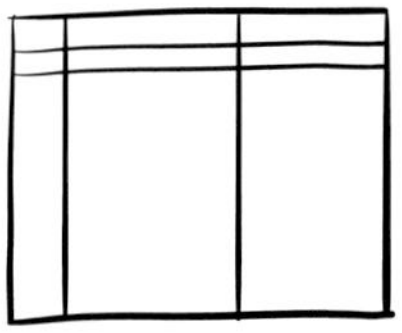

Plans

Big-View: You evaluate product options and select the ones that you anticipate will yield high value during the next several years. The candidate solutions include features identified on a product roadmap.

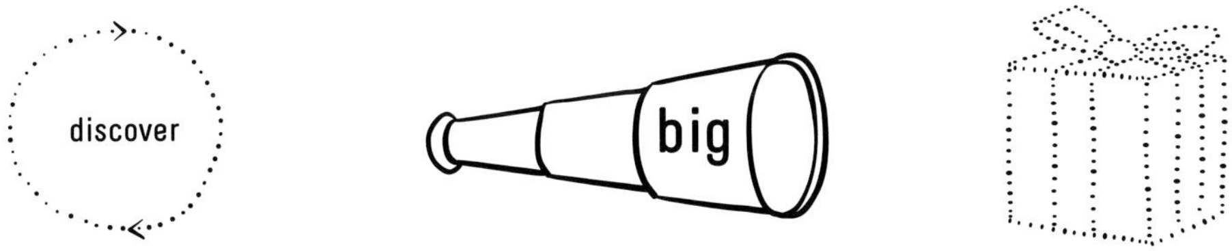

Pre-View: You evaluate and select the product options for the next delivery cycle, perhaps one to twelve weeks. The candidate solutions may be one or more stories or MMFs on a release plan.

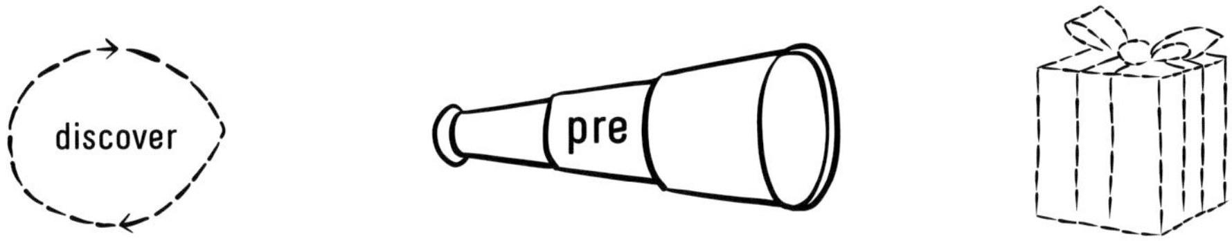

Now-View: You evaluate product options and select the ones for immediate development and potential delivery. The candidate solutions may be one or more stories or MMFs.

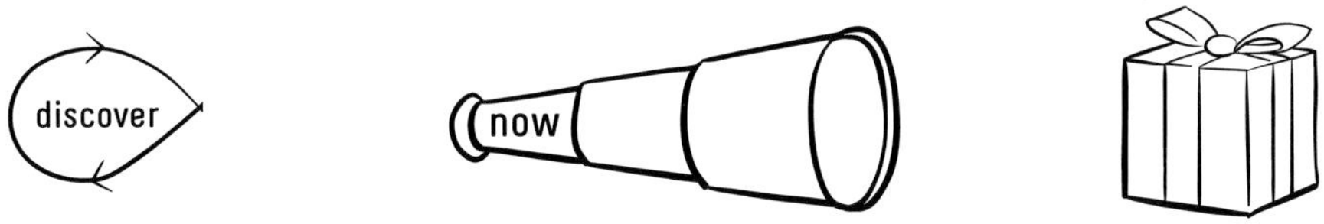

Weighing Benefits and Risks

When evaluating the product options, you weigh the impact of benefits and risks. For example, you might lower the value of a risky option, or you might choose to incur risks, hoping to achieve a higher benefit. *External risks* include those related to customers, markets, and regulations. *Internal risks* are related to the people and technologies involved in delivering the product.

Consider the risk of lost value if you mistakenly deliver solutions to customers in combinations that the customers don't need or can't use (yet). Or, if you deliver an option too late, you risk losing market share, customer goodwill, and reputation. It's also important to consider team and technology risks. Team considerations include team domain knowledge, technical skills, access to subject matter experts and customer feedback, the strength of the team's cohesiveness and collaboration ("team jell"), familiarity with the technologies, and team members' physical access to each other (whether they are co-located or distributed).

Using distributed teams working from different locations can have a significant impact. One remedy is to have people in each location work on a solution that is highly cohesive and has minimal dependencies on the work of other teams. In this way you minimize misunderstanding and reduce the risk of rework.

Evaluating Dependencies

You strive to identify the optimal sequence for candidate solutions—one that achieves maximum value as soon as possible. To do this, you evaluate both external and internal (or product) dependencies. That is, you determine whether the order of delivering one solution before another solution will enhance or threaten value. You may have to defer delivering a candidate solution that has external dependencies, for example, when your candidate solution relies on an external system or deliverables from other parties (people, teams, external business partners).

Internal product dependencies occur when a candidate solution relies on another part of the product—for example, data created in an interface. You can evaluate internal dependencies by using *dependency graphs*, interaction matrices, and the like. These tools help you visualize dependencies and adjust your delivery sequences accordingly.

The Timing of Evaluation

You evaluate product options continually throughout the product's life cycle. Continual evaluation lets you respond to changing customer and market needs, technologies, and business strategies.

The timing and frequency of evaluation can vary based on the team's delivery method. Evaluation might follow a predictable cadence, such as daily, every two weeks, monthly, or quarterly. Or you can evaluate options on demand whenever the queue is open. Some teams use a combination approach.

You can also vary the length of the time for allocating candidate solutions. If you're using timebox delivery, you might deploy candidate solutions using a regular cadence. The length of the timeframe (monthly, quarterly) will drive the number of candidate solutions you allocate to each delivery cycle.

Another technique is to evaluate product options in daily stand-up meetings, informal discussions, or facilitated workshops. When you're evaluating and allocating product options to longer time horizons, it's a good idea to use well-planned, facilitated workshops.

Encouraging Critical Thinking

Evaluating options and candidate solutions requires a critical, analytic approach. Here are questions that encourage critical thinking:

- Which options best fit the theme or goal of the next delivery cycle?
- Which options might provide the highest value to upcoming market or seasonal time cycles? Which options are necessary for the organization to be competitive?
- How does one option (versus another one) fit into the overall product roadmap?
- Which options provide the greater market penetration? Which might have higher customer value due to newness, presenting a market opportunity?
- Which options might gain value if they are tackled earlier and the partners learn more about associated risks?

Confirm

You check the product before, during, and after delivery.

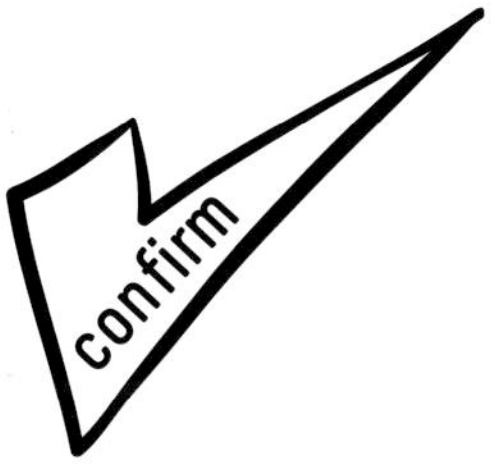

What kind of evidence can you use to verify the expected outcomes of the upcoming delivery?
What results show you that the delivered solution was implemented correctly?
How can you validate that the solution meets your business objectives?
How will you learn whether you delivered the right solution?

Confirm to Learn

The structured conversation isn't over until the partners confirm their shared expectations for the candidate solution. This confirmation enhances the partners' understanding of the product options.

You use acceptance criteria (also called *conditions of satisfaction, doneness criteria,* or doneness tests) to verify and validate the candidate solution. Acceptance criteria provide concrete, unambiguous, measureable means to confirm that the candidate solution's outcomes are correct. Acceptance criteria guide development and testing.

You define acceptance criteria during discovery as a way to elicit and clarify product needs. These same acceptance criteria are used during delivery to guide development and testing to verify you are correctly building the candidate solution.

The candidate solution is a speculation or investment proposal that you believe will achieve business value. Therefore, you continually validate its actual results against business objectives. During discovery, actual results from prior deliveries are considered as you evaluate product options. During delivery, demonstrations and user acceptance testing validate that your candidate solution is ready for release.

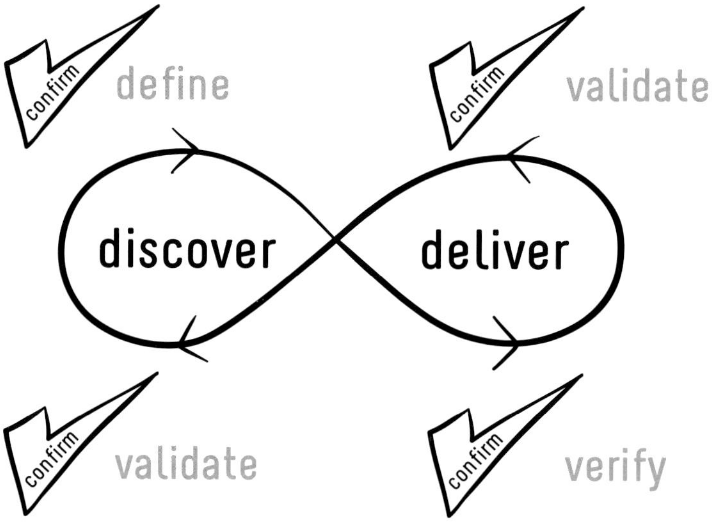

Confirm to Learn

Consider your candidate solution to be a hypothesis that enables validated learning (Reis, 2011). The partners confirm that their candidate solution is valuable and meets the right customers' needs—*customer validation* (Blank, 2005). It's essential to measure the solution's actual results. Confirm objectives as quickly as possible to speed your learning, especially if your product is a startup.

Specifying Acceptance Criteria

Acceptance criteria may take the form of text descriptions, scenarios, checklists, examples, specifications, or tests. As you define acceptance criteria, you often discover additional options, which in turn need to be explored. These same acceptance criteria may also be valuable for documenting the product, especially for regulatory compliance.

The granularity and specificity of acceptance criteria vary depending on planning view. Now-View acceptance criteria are the most precise, specific, testable, Pre-View less precise and specific, and Big-View the least precise, specific.

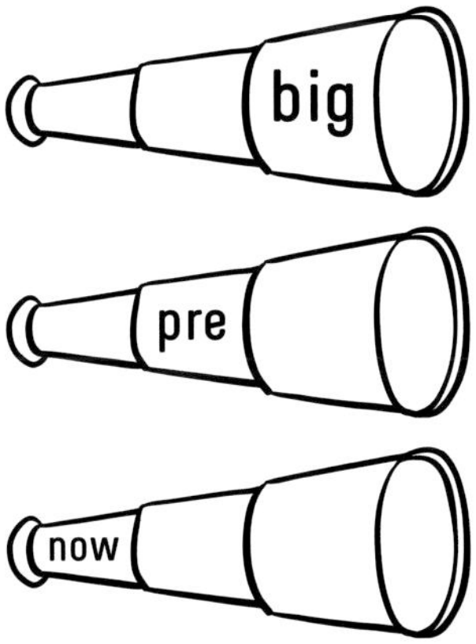

	Product Capabilities	Examples	Acceptance Criteria
big	Wants	Feature	Scenario
pre	Needs	MMF, Story	Acceptance criteria list
now	Requirements	Story	Given-When-Then, Data examples, Planguage

Acceptance Criteria by View

Explore and Evaluate the 7 Product Dimensions: A Detailed Guide

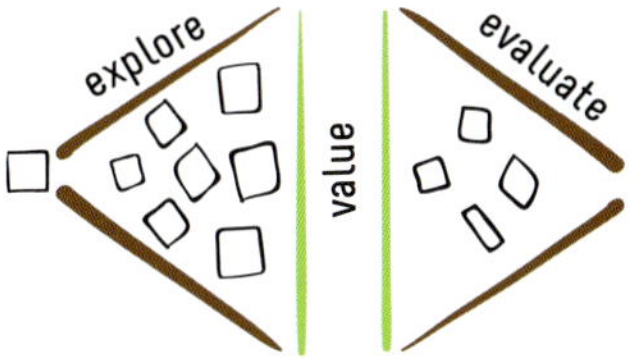

Our subject is the feature "Optimize Scheduling" from Squeeky Kleen's product roadmap (Section 1, Case Study, Big-View).

	User	Interface	Action	Data	Control	Environment	Quality Attribute
Page	129	135	141	149	157	163	171

?	A discovery question you may ask
(pen)	Points to a useful Tool or Technique (Section 6)
Don't Forget	Additional tips for exploring and evaluating the dimension

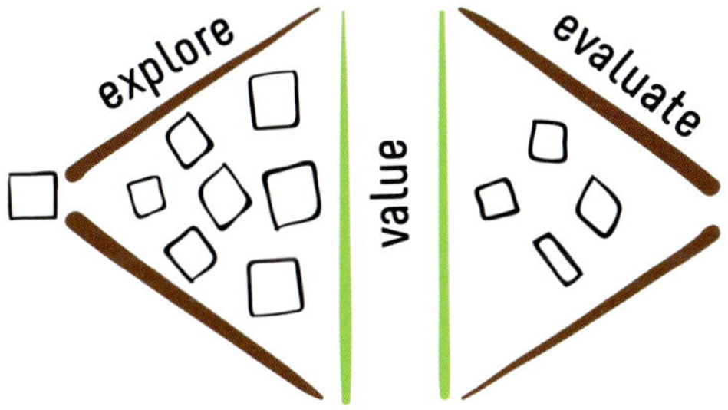

User

1. User options
2. User state options
3. User role options

1. User options

1.a. Explore user options for the current view of the product.

? What users engage with the product?

SK User Options
- Cleaner
- Customer
- CSR
- Inventory Manager
- Sales Manager

? Who initiates actions, and what are their goals?
Who receives output from the system?
Who participates in fulfilling actions?

Context Diagram

Draw a context diagram to visualize the users' interactions with the product.

Persona

Learn more about key users' needs and goals by creating personas.

1.b. Evaluate user options by referencing the goals, objectives, and value considerations.

Cleaner

Benefit: Cleaners spend approximately 10% of their time using software tools.

Decision: For this delivery cycle, cleaners will continue to use their existing tools.

Customer

Benefit: Without customers SK would go out of business!

Decision: For this delivery cycle, include support for customers.

CSR

Benefit: CSRs spend all their time in the office supporting customer requests. They need a variety of software tools to improve their efficiency.

Decision: For this delivery cycle, support CSRs.

2. User state options

2.a. Explore the user state options for high-value users.

? For each option, are there specific life cycle states?

CSR state options:

- Senior
- Junior
- Trainee

2.b. Evaluate user state options by referencing the goals, objectives, and value considerations.

CSR states

Trainee state

Benefit: Reduce one-on-one training provided by junior and senior CSRs.

Junior state

Benefit: Majority of the CSRs are junior.

Senior state

Risk: Complexity of their work will require significant analysis and development.

Decision: For this delivery cycle, support the junior CSR state.

3. User role options

3.a. Explore the *user role* options for high-value users.

? What roles do users play?

User: CSR

User role options

- Estimator
- Service Scheduler
- Job Canceler
- Job Rescheduler
- Job Reminder

User Role Map

User roles can be illustrated in a user role map.

3.b. Evaluate user role options by referencing the goals, objectives, and value considerations.

Service Scheduler role

- Benefit: CSRs spend most of their time scheduling jobs.
- Decision: For this delivery cycle, focus on Service Scheduler.

Results of the User Dimension Analysis

High-value options that will be included in this delivery cycle are noted with a star (*).

User Options	User State Options	User Role Options
Cleaner		
Customer*	New Existing*	
CSR*	Senior Junior* Trainee	Estimator Service Scheduler* Job Canceler Job Rescheduler Job Reminder
Inventory Manager		
Sales Manager		

Don't Forget

Exploring Users

Look for user options in:

- Vision statement, list of goals and objectives
- Glossary terms that represent people or organizations
- List of partners who are users
- Marketing materials targeting a persona
- Roles that: install and maintain the software; start up and shut down the system software; provide training on how to use the system software; provide help desk support.
- Use a variety of models to explore user options.

  User Role Map, Business Process Diagram, Context Diagram, Prototype

Naming Users

- Use business terms.
- To name the initiating user role, use a name that reflects the user's intention in using the system—typically, the action verb adjusted to end with "-er" or "-or."

  A CSR who estimates services could be named "Estimator."

  A CSR who reschedules jobs could be named "Job Rescheduler."
- Define your high-value user options in your glossary.

  Glossary

Evaluating Users

When you're evaluating user options, consider:

Alignment with strategy

  Represents an underserved market

  Alignment with market segmentation strategy

  Potential to be an influential user (to influence others to use or buy the product)

  Customer loyalty

Goals, motivations

  Key drivers for using the product

Demographics
- Native language
- Familiarity with technology
- Familiarity with domain

Usage
- Current number of users
- Frequency and regularity of user interactions with the product
  - per minute/hour/day/week/month/quarter/year
- Expected growth rate—number of users and frequency of use
- Duration of user interaction with the product
- Data about user states and roles

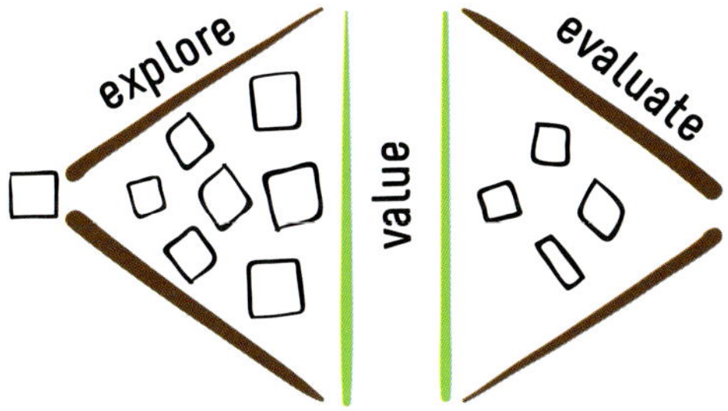

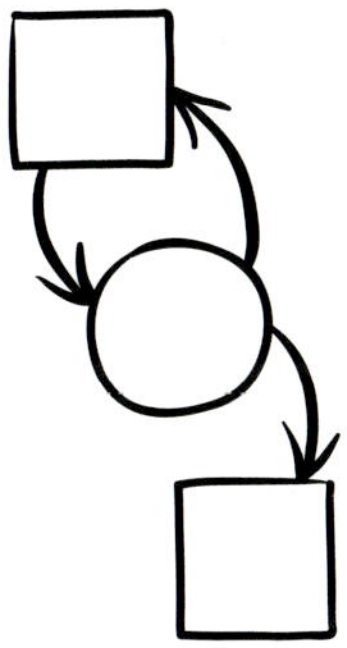

Interface

1. Interface options
2. Interface status and type options

1. Interface options

1.a. Explore options for the current view of the product.

? What interfaces are needed to send data or messages to or from the product?

SK Scheduling interface options

Customer provides service request details.
SK sends a customer a confirmation that the job has been scheduled.
SK sends Inventory a reservation for special equipment.
Cleaner requests job details.
SK sends a customer a reminder about an upcoming job.
Customer provides sign-off after the job is completed.

? Which users initiate sending data to the product? Which users receive data from the product?
(Reminder: the term "user" may refer to a person, an interacting system, or a hardware device.)

Context Diagram

Draw a context diagram to visualize the interfaces and users.

? Is a given interface unique due to user options?

CSRs and cleaners have many similar interface needs, and there are some differences that need to be explored.

? Does an interface have unique data due to data type?

Window cleaning services and solar panel cleaning have some distinct data attributes that will affect the interface.

? Which environments expand or limit your interface options for the next delivery cycles?

Customers may contact SK from any location.

Cleaners typically work outside the SK office 90% of the time during regular business hours.

? Which quality attributes affect your options for the next delivery cycles?

Ease of use is key for all users, but that means different things to new users versus experienced ones.

1.b. Evaluate the interface options by referencing the goals, objectives, and value considerations.

SK sends a customer a reminder about an upcoming job.

Benefit of interface: Cuts down the number of "not at home" problems when the cleaner arrives onsite.
Especially important if the cleaner needs access to the property to complete services (e.g., interior cleaning).

Decision: For this delivery cycle, provide interface.

Cleaner looks up job details.

Benefit of interface: Cleaner needs to know the job details to adequately prepare.

Decision: For this delivery cycle, provide interface.

Prototype

Consider prototyping high-value interfaces.

2. Interface status and type options

2.a. Explore the high-value interfaces' status and type options.

? What is the status of the interface?

New or existing

? What are the interface type options?

User interface

Auditory (voice, interactive voice recognition), speech, graphical user interfaces (GUIs), touch, direct manipulation, eye tracking, etc.

System-to-system

Hardware device

2.b. Evaluate the interfaces' status and type options by referencing the goals, objectives, and value considerations.

Customer provides service request details using a new user interface.

Benefit of new interface: Improve operational efficiencies and data accuracy.

Risks of new interface: It is unclear how willing existing customers will be to use the new interface.

Amount of time needed for design and usability testing.

Decision: For this delivery cycle, continue with current mode: customers communicating their requests through CSRs.

System sends customer a job reminder using a new user interface.

Benefit of adding another interface: Many customers have asked to receive reminders about their upcoming job via a text message.

Decision: For this delivery cycle, provide additional user interface.

Customer signs off on completed job using cleaner's new handheld device.

Benefit: Eliminates paper shuffling; the job's status is updated immediately.

Risk: Dependent on exploring and selecting appropriate device and integrating it with SK databases.
Operationally, situations where a customer is not available or is unable to use the device.

Decision: For this delivery cycle, continue with current paper sign-off process.

Results of Interface Dimension Analysis

Interfaces	Currently	Type options	
		Wish	Next delivery cycle
Customer provides service request details	Phone	GUI	No change
SK sends a customer a confirmation that the job has been scheduled	Email	Text message	Provide text message interface
SK sends Inventory a reservation for special equipment	Paper	System-to-system	No change
Cleaner looks up job details	Phone	GUI	No change
SK sends a customer a reminder about an upcoming job	Phone	GUI, text message	Provide text message interface
Customer provides sign-off after job is completed	Paper	Handheld device	No change

Don't Forget

Exploring Interfaces

- Use a variety of models to explore the interface options.

  Context Diagram, Prototype, *Relationship Map*, Business Process Diagram

Evaluating Interfaces

When you're evaluating interface options, consider:

Alignment with strategy

  Market and organizational readiness

  Competitive positioning

  Customer experience, usability

Dependency

  Interfacing with other systems

  Hardware and software

  For user interfaces, the operational environment, mobility

Usage

  Current tools used (phones, documents, software, tools, instruments)

Financial implications

  For user interfaces—cost of usability testing, training costs

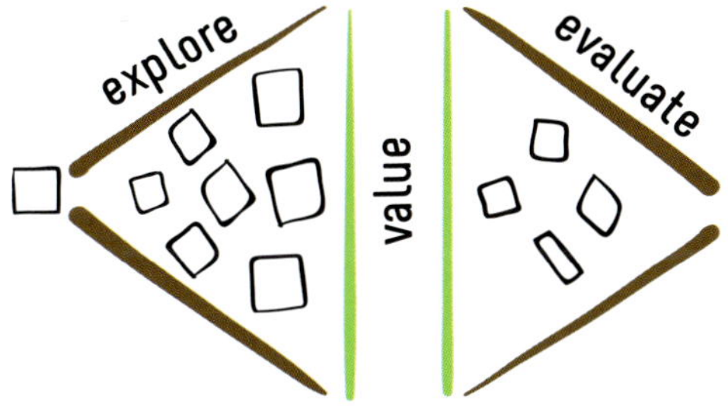

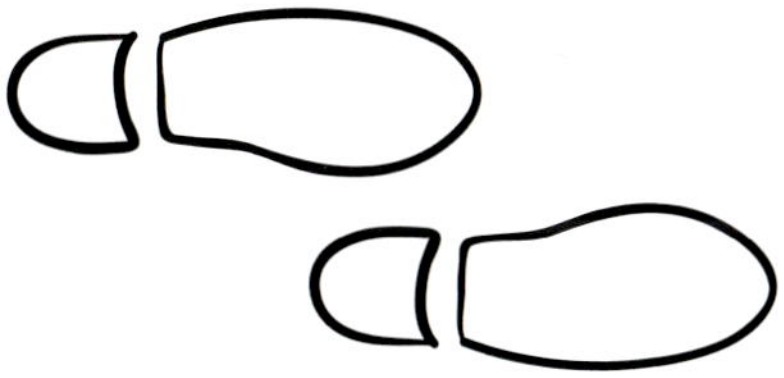

Action

1. Action options

1.a. Explore action options for the current view of the product.
How can you gauge an action's level of detail?

In the Big-View: A Big-View action, typically called a process, spans a "beginning-to-end" *value stream*, triggered by an event.

SK Process Options

- Provide Estimates
- Schedule Services
- Manage Inventory
- Conduct Sales Activities

In the Pre-View: A Pre-View action is a set of interrelated responses, initiated by an event, that produces a specific valued result for the user. You can write such actions using short, active verb-object phrases (e.g., "search for services"), or you can describe these actions in sentence form.

Triggering Events	Action Response Options	
	Short form	Sentence form
Customer wants to learn about SK services and locations.	Search for services and locations.	As a customer, I need to search for services so...
Customer contacts SK to arrange for services.	Schedule a job.	As a customer, I need to schedule cleaning services so...
Cleaner reports the job is completed.	Complete a job.	As a cleaner, I need to notify the office that the job is completed so...
Time to order supplies.	Order supplies.	As the Inventory Manager, I need to replenish supplies so...
Time to follow up with customer.	Request feedback on services.	As the Sales Manager, I need to get feedback on recently provided services so...

In the Now-View: At the lowest level, a Now-View action is an atomic, indivisible response to an event.

Schedule a Job: Action Options

- Verify that requested location is within SK service area.
- Verify that requested service is provided by SK.
- Calculate price for requested services.
- Confirm price with customer.
- Find available cleaner to perform service.
- Verify payment method.
- Verify credit card details.
- Confirm job details with customer.
- Reserve any special equipment.
- Store job details.
- Send job confirmation to customer.
- Provide cancellation policy to customer.
- Provide liability policy to customer.

Explore the timing and flow of the actions.

? When does this action occur?
Must the action be done at the same time as other actions, or does it provide value when done by itself?
How do the actions flow?
What is the sequence of the actions?

Big-View and Pre-View: The product champion explains the typical flow: a customer schedules a job, the cleaner completes the job, then SK requests feedback on the services.

Pre-View and Now-View: The product champion explains there is no value in trying to find an available cleaner to perform the service until we confirm the price with the customer.

Business Process Diagram
Visualize the flow of the actions using a business process diagram.

Story Map
You can use a story map to organize stories. Arrange the stories from left to right based on sequence of usage; top to bottom based on value (higher value near the top).

Explore action dependencies.

? What are the preconditions of the action options?

Reschedule, Cancel, and Complete job are all dependent on a Job being scheduled. Their precondition is "job is scheduled," which is the postcondition of Schedule job.

Dependency Graph
Visualize the process, feature, or story dependencies on a dependency graph.

1.b. Evaluate the action options by referencing the goals, objectives, and value considerations.

Schedule a job

Benefits: Scheduling jobs is what the CSRs spend most of their time doing. SK's financial stream begins with scheduling jobs. Scheduling must be as efficient and effective as possible.

Risk: Big learning curve for CSRs to transition to new application.

Decision: For this delivery cycle, the automated system that the CSRs use will include basic, easy-to-learn scheduling capabilities.

Reschedule a job

Benefit: Customers want flexibility to quickly change the date or time of a job.

Risks: Inability to reschedule could lead to losing customers. Fewer than 10% of jobs are rescheduled.

Decision: For this delivery cycle, continue to use existing manual rescheduling.

Verify that requested location is within SK service area.
Verify that requested service is provided by SK.
Calculate price for requested services.

Benefit: These three actions are already in use for Provide Estimate.

Decision: For this delivery cycle, reuse what has been done for estimating.

Find available cleaner to perform service.

Benefit: Quickly scheduling a cleaner is key to completing the customer's request.

Risk: Understanding which cleaner is available is complex due to vacations, sick days, and skills needed for a particular job.

Decision: For this delivery cycle, continue to use existing manual scheduling.

Results of the Action Dimension Analysis

High-value options that will be included in this delivery cycle are noted with a star (*).

Event	Action Options	Detailed Action Options
Customer contacts SK to arrange for services.*	Provide estimate	
	Schedule a job*	Verify that requested location is within SK service area.* Verify that requested service is provided by SK.* Calculate price for requested services.* Confirm price with customer.* Find available cleaner to perform service.* Verify payment method. Verify credit card details. Confirm job details with customer.* Reserve any needed special equipment. Store job details.* Send job confirmation to customer.* Provide cancellation policy to customer. Provide liability policy to customer.
Customer needs to reschedule the job. Cleaner calls in sick.	Reschedule a job	
Customer decides to cancel a job.*	Cancel a job*	Compare canceled date and time with SK's cancellation terms. Assess any cancellation fee. Update job status.*
Cleaner reports the job is completed.	Complete a job	
Time to order supplies.	Order supplies	
Time to follow up with customer.	Follow up on completed job Follow up on canceled job	

Don't Forget

Exploring Actions

Look for action options in:

- Vision statement, list of goals and objectives
- Marketing materials, features
- Product backlog
- Vendor software package documentation

Use a variety of models to explore action options.

Business Process Diagram, *Capability Map*, Dependency Graph, Story Map, *Use Case, Value Stream Map*

- Observe people as they engage with the product.

Examine scenarios.

Scenario Z Pattern

- Scenarios at the Big-View lead you to actions for the Pre-View.
- Scenarios at the Pre-View lead you to actions for the Now-View.
- Scenarios at the Now-View lead you to user acceptance tests.

Consider MMFs *(minimum marketable features).*

MMF

- Top down: slice features into smallest possible subset that delivers value.
- Bottom up: cluster stories to ensure significant value.

Writing Actions

- Write events using this syntax: initiating user + active verb + noun phrase (e.g., Customer needs to cancel a job).
- Write actions using an active verb + noun phrase (e.g., Cancel a scheduled job).
- Story formats:

  As a <user>, I need to <action verb> so I can <business benefit>

  or

  In order to <business value> as a <user> I need to <action verb>

- Nouns in action phrases should be business domain terms that are defined in the glossary or the *data dictionary*.

Glossary, Data Dictionary

- Distinguish actions from controls. Here's an action: Verify credit card payment. In contrast, a control is a constraint to be enforced: Payment by credit cards may be made only if the customer's credit score is 600 or higher.

Evaluating Actions

When you're evaluating action options, consider:

Flow and Dependency
- Sequence of actions
- Whether an action is dependent on another action or on preexisting data

Usage
- Current execution—per minute/hour/day/week/month/quarter/year
- Peak periods
- Expected growth rate
- Location of execution
- Critical, noncritical; audited, not audited; compliance, non-compliance

State of existing actions
- Automated, non-automated, combination

Automation
- Financial cost
- Impact on people, organization

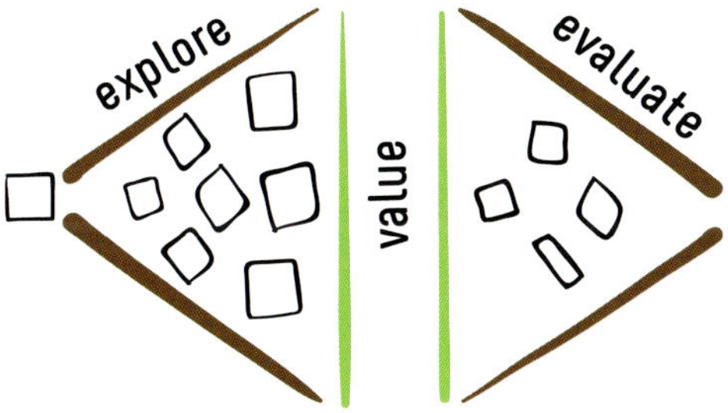

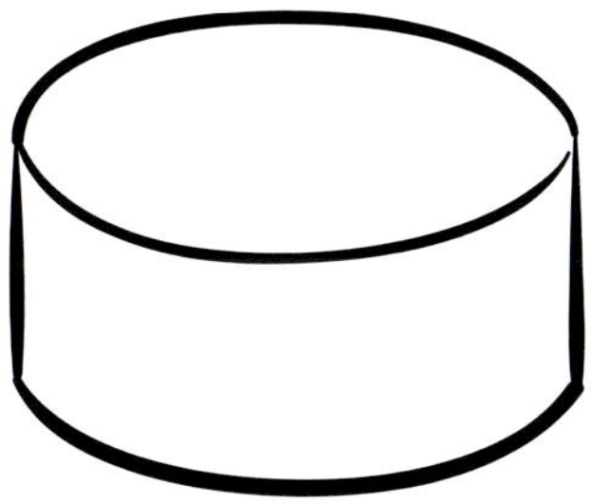

Data

1. Data and relationship options
2. Data type options
3. Data state options
4. Data attribute options

1. Data and relationship options

1.a. Explore data and relationship options for the current view of the product.

? What data must be represented in the product?

What data is created, read, updated, or deleted by the product's actions?

List the data options.

SK Data Options

- Cleaner
- Customer
- Deposit
- Job
- Payment
- Property
- Property Type
- Service Area
- Window Type

Data Dictionary, *Data Entity*

? What are the relationships among the data options?

List the relationship options.

Customer contracts for a job

Cleaner scheduled for a job

Customer prefers a cleaner

Data Model: *Conceptual Data Model*

Visualize the data relationships in a data model.

Further define your *data relationships'* cardinality and optionality.

? Cardinality: How many instances of one entity can be related to the other entity?

Relationship: Customer contracts for a job.

Many: Customer can contract for many jobs. SK likes these kinds of customers!

Relationship: Job contracted with a customer.

One: A job is contracted with a maximum of one customer. SK has learned the hard way that it wants to deal with only one customer for a job.

? Optionality: Is the relationship optional or mandatory?

Relationship: Customer contracts for a job.

Optional: A customer is independent of a job. This means that data about a customer can be remembered by SK even if that person has never scheduled a job. For example, the marketing department occasionally buys lists of prospective customers.

Relationship: Job contracted with a customer.

Mandatory: A job is dependent on a customer. In other words, SK would never capture data about a job if it cannot associate the job with a specific customer.

You may write the relationships as sentences using a data relationship template.

Each ____________ may/must ___________ one/one or more___________.
entity A verb entity B

Each customer may contract for one or more jobs.
Each job must be contracted with one customer.

Alternatively (or in addition), add the notation to the data model.

Data Model: *Logical Data Model*

? Is a relationship transferable over time as result of some action?
Can a job be reassigned to a different cleaner?
Yes, but only if the job is in the "estimated," "scheduled," or "incomplete" state.

1.b. Evaluate the data and relationship options by referencing the goals, objectives, and value considerations.

Job
Benefit: Data about a job is key to providing excellent customer service.
Decision: For this delivery cycle, job data must be implemented.

Deposit
Benefit: Requiring deposits for certain jobs helps to control financial losses by SK.
Risks: Deposit data must comply with external regulations, e.g., local governing authorities. Deposits are low risk because only a small percentage of SK's jobs require a deposit.
Decision: For this delivery cycle, the application will not support scheduling jobs that require a deposit. A job that requires a deposit will be scheduled by a senior CSR.

2. Data state options

2.a. Explore the data *state* options for high-value data (domain, entity, entity type) options.

? For each option, are there specific life cycle states?

Customer state options	Job state options
active	scheduled
inactive	canceled
	completed
	paid
	signed-off
	unfinished

State Diagram

Sketch a state diagram. Use the diagram to explore the allowable transitions from one state to another.

2. b. Evaluate the data state options by referencing the goals, objectives, and value considerations.

Job states

All job states

Benefit: Enables timely, complete, and accurate reporting.

Canceled job state

Benefit: Can reschedule the cleaner, decrease amount of downtime.

Completed job state

Benefit: Can invoice customer as soon as possible.

Decision: For this delivery cycle, support scheduled and canceled job states.

3. Data type options

3.a. Explore data type options (if any) for high-value data options.

? Are there unique types of a data option?

The Product Champion explains that a customer could be a person, or it could be an organization that contracts for services with SK.

The common characteristics are encapsulated in the *supertype* "customer." Any unique data, relationships, or both are modeled in the *subtypes*. For example, an individual customer has a first and last name whereas an organizational customer has a business name, resulting in subtypes "individual customer" and "organizational customer." This abstraction of the supertype and specialization of the subtypes is key for the flexible future extension of the product.

Data Model: *Inheritance Hierarchy*
Visualize the types using an inheritance hierarchy

3.b. Evaluate data type options by referencing the goals, objectives, and value considerations.

Customer types
- Individual customer
  - Benefit: This is SK's existing business base.
- Organizational customer
  - Risks: This is dependent on the Sales Manager researching and analyzing competitive pricing. Will require supporting additional window types. Also may require additional data to support multiple contacts within an organization (e.g., contracts administrator, building maintenance staff).

Decision: For this delivery cycle, support individual customer.

4. Data attribute options

4.a. Explore data attribute options for high-value data (entity, entity type, entity state).

? What specific data is needed?

For a canceled job, SK captures the reason that the job was canceled, by whom (customer or SK), date and time, and any related penalty.

? Must an attribute contain a value?

The canceled date is null unless the job is canceled.

? Is an attribute limited to a set of predefined values?

The job status must be either scheduled, unfinished, completed, canceled, paid, or signed-off.

Data Dictionary

Use a data dictionary or logical data model to capture attribute details.

4.b. Evaluate the data attribute options by referencing the goals, objectives, and value considerations.

Canceled job attribute options

Benefit of capturing a job's cancellation attributes:

Management needs to analyze cancellations and identify ways to reduce them.

Decision: For this delivery cycle, capture the job cancellation attributes.

Results of Data Dimension Analysis

High-value options that will be included in this delivery cycle are noted with a star (*).

Data	Types	States	Attributes
Cleaner			
Customer*	individual* organization	active* inactive	(individual-active)* first name* last name* email phone number
Deposit			
Job*		scheduled* unfinished completed canceled* paid signed-off	(scheduled)* scheduled date* scheduled time* status* comments (canceled)* canceled date* canceled time* canceled reason* canceled penalty*
Payment			
Property*			street* city* state* postal code*
Service Area*			postal code*
Window Type*			name* description cleaning price*

Don't Forget

Exploring Data

- Look for nouns that represent data options in:
  - Vision statement, list of goals and objectives
  - Glossary terms that represent data that must be saved
  - Legacy databases: reverse-engineer databases to aid planning and analysis
- Use a variety of models to explore data options.

Data Model, State Diagram

Naming Data

- Use business terms.
- Define your domain and data entity options in your glossary; define attributes in a data dictionary.

Glossary, Data Dictionary

Evaluating Data

When you're evaluating data options, consider:

Source
- Current, future
- Internal, external

State of data
- Automated, non-automated, combination
- Quality
- Integrity
- Synchronized
- Internationalized or localized

Dependency
- Data that is dependent on other data
- Data needed by an action or control option
- Data dependent on another source (system)

Usage
- Frequency, peak periods
- Critical, noncritical
- Audited, not audited
- Compliance, non-compliance

Volume
- Current volume
- Expected growth rate
- Retention

Security
- Authorization levels
- Privacy

Compliance
- Laws
- Standards

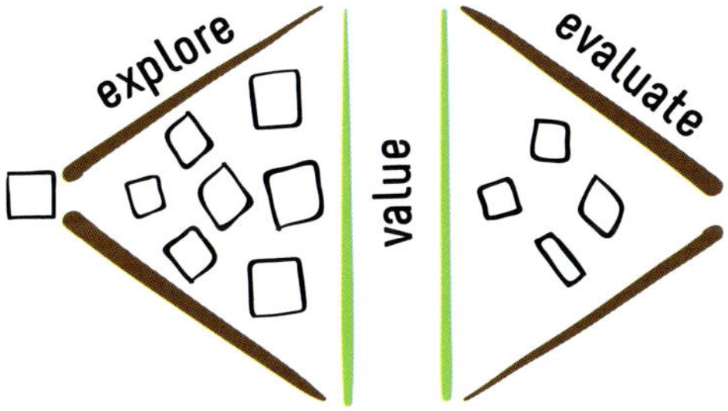

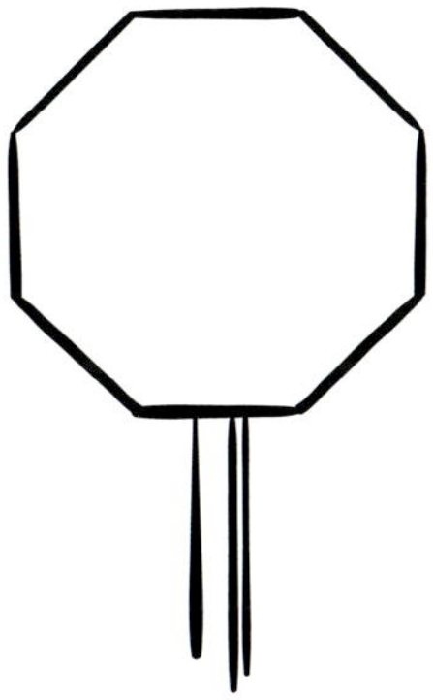

Control

1. Control option

1.a. Explore the control options for the current view of the product.

? Are there control options that are unique to the high-value user's state, role, or both?

Only a junior or senior CSR is allowed to cancel a job.

? Are there control options that must be enforced by high-value actions?

Action	Control Option
Verify that requested service is provided by SK.	A requested service must match a service currently offered by SK.

? Are there specific control options for the high-value data's type and or state?

Business policy: A customer who has not paid for prior services may be prevented from scheduling new services.

Business rule: An individual customer whose total delinquent payment amount is greater than $250 must not schedule new services.

Data Model, Inheritance Hierarchy, State Diagram
To discover more control options, review visuals of the data types and states.

Consider additional details for each control option that may influence the evaluation.

? Which stakeholder specifies the control?
Is that stakeholder internal or external to the organization?

? What is the jurisdiction level?
Will the control be enforced universally? Or will it be limited to:
Business location—geographical boundary
Organizational boundary

? What is the enforcement level?
Can the control be overridden (that is, is it merely a guideline)?
If it can be overridden, who is authorized to do so? Is this a new user role?

Control Statement	Source	Jurisdiction	Enforcement Level
SK must collect taxes for all services it provides.	External governing body	Local, regional	Strict
A requested location (postal code) must be within an area supported by SK on the requested service date.	SK	Global	Strict
A job canceled less than one business day prior to the job's scheduled date must be charged a cancellation fee.	SK	Regional	Override

? Are the controls part of a set?

The rules for providing a discount are based on the type of property and the amount of the customer's total paid services in the past 12 calendar months.

Discount of 0% for a residential property with total paid services >$250

Discount of 3% for a residential property with total paid services >$499

Decision Table, Decision Tree

Use a decision table or decision tree to visualize the controls. (Controls may be implemented as data parameters that can be modified without recoding or recompiling the product.)

1.b. Evaluate the control options by referencing the goals, objectives, and value considerations.

? Is it necessary to enforce every control option and enforce it consistently?

Is it possible and feasible to enforce every control option?

Is there a consequence to non-compliance?

Which control options could be enforced by software or manually?

Control option: A customer with a total delinquent payment amount greater than a specified value must not schedule new services.

Benefit: Limit the amount of potentially uncollectible payments.

Risk: The data needed to determine the delinquent payment amount is not readily available.

Decision: For this delivery cycle, work with Finance to craft a manual work-around that prevents the "top 5 delinquent customers" from scheduling new services.

Results of Control Dimension Analysis

High-value options that will be included in this delivery cycle are noted with a star (*).

Policy and Regulation Group Options	Policy and Regulation Options	Business Rule Options
Schedule a job*	A customer who has not paid for prior services may be prevented from scheduling new services.	An individual customer whose total delinquent payment amount is greater than $250 must not schedule new services.
	A requested service must match a service currently offered by SK.*	The requested service date must be equal to or greater than the service availability date.*
		A requested service location (postal code) must be within an area supported by SK on the requested service date.*
	A cleaner must not be double-booked.	A cleaner must not be scheduled for more than one job for the same date and time.
Cancel a job*	A cancellation may be assessed a cancellation fee.	A job canceled less than one business day prior to the Job's date of service must be charged a cancellation fee.*

Don't Forget!

Exploring Controls

- Look for control options in goals and objectives.
- Check for partners (customers, advisers, regulators) who "own" business policies and rules—for example, a local governing body that defines sales taxes.
- Use visuals to explore control options.

Decision Table, Decision Tree

Writing Controls

- Nouns in control statements should be business domain terms defined in the glossary or the data dictionary.

Glossary, Data Dictionary

- Write policies and regulations as general statements using business domain terms.
- Write as a statement, not an action.
  Control: *Payment by credit card may be made only if the customer's credit score is 600 or higher.*
  Action statement (syntax: active verb + noun phrase): *Verify credit card payment.*
- A testable business rule is written as an atomic statement, meaning that it cannot be divided into smaller parts without losing meaning. It may be written as an executable test.
- When written at the atomic level, testable business rules may serve as the basis for error messages. Example: *The requested service date must be equal to or greater than the service availability date.*
- You can use decision tables or decision trees to define sets of business rules.

Decision Table, Decision Tree

Evaluating Controls

When you're evaluating control options, consider:

- Source
  - Internal, external
- State of existing controls
  - Automated, non-automated, combination
  - Quality
  - Internationalized or localized
- Jurisdiction
  - Geographical boundary, organizational boundary
- Enforcement
  - Strict, override, override with authorization, guideline
- Liability
  - Ensure compliance with regulations
  - Protect organization from harm
  - Protect customer from harm

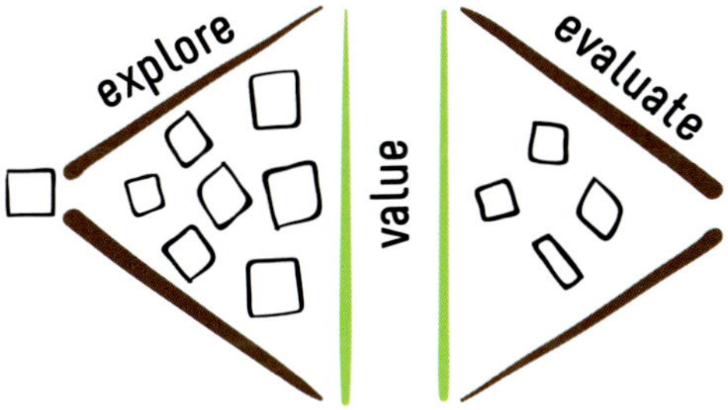

Environment

1. **Physical properties**
2. **Technology platform**

1. Physical property options

1.a. Explore the physical property options of the product.

? What are the locations where users will operate the product?
What is the physical place and space like?

Users	Location
Cleaner	On-site, inside and outside customer's property SK office Supply warehouse Vehicle
CSR	Off-site SK office
Inventory Manager	Supply warehouse
Sales Manager	Off-site SK office Vehicle

? What are the physical conditions surrounding users when they interact with the product? Are there considerations such as lighting, noise, temperature, weather conditions, and proximity to other machines or people?

Users	Locations	Physical Conditions
Cleaner	On-site, inside and outside customer's property SK office Supply warehouse Vehicle	Primarily outside, under variable weather conditions No dedicated space No temperature control Cramped
CSR	Off-site SK office	Variable networked space Noisy, shared, congested office space
Inventory Manager	Supply warehouse	No temperature control
Sales Manager	Off-site SK office Vehicle	Variable networked space Private office space Cramped

? What are the product's properties that the users can see or perceive, such as size, space, height, width, weight, energy, color, smell, finish, labeling, appearance, style, packaging, space utilization? What are the options for the product's form and finish?

Users	Locations	Physical Conditions	Composition
Cleaner	On-site, inside and outside customer's property	Primarily outside, under variable weather conditions	Handheld device. Must fit in one hand, weight not to exceed 4lbs. Four-hour battery life.

? For a physical product, what are the product's internal property options, such as memory usage, energy consumption, and utilization such as heat and pressure?

? How will users interact with the product? What mechanisms will be used for inputting, choosing, viewing, or otherwise using the product? Will there be visual, touch, or auditory modes of interactions? How will the product be installed, revised, configured, licensed, adapted, protected, and, when no longer in use, how will the users dispose of the product?

Users	Locations	Physical Conditions	Composition	Access Modes
Cleaner	On-site, inside and outside customer's property.	Primarily outside, under variable weather conditions.	Handheld mobile device. Must fit in one hand, weight not to exceed 4 lbs. Four-hour battery life.	Touchscreen, pen, vibrate, auditory confirmation with max 105 decibels, average 80 decibels.

1.b. Evaluate the physical property options by referencing the goals, objectives, and value considerations.

Cleaner on-site at customer property using handheld mobile device
- Benefits: Estimate can be shared with the SK office immediately without paper transport.
  Job can be scheduled at the time of estimating without callbacks and with fewer errors.
  SK can obtain payment immediately after job completion.
  Customer can immediately schedule the next job.
  Customer can receive invoice upon completion of job.
- Risks: Cleaners have developed habits for manual quotes, may be reluctant to add another device to the set of supplies they must prepare before going to customer property. Cleaners have different levels of proficiency with handheld devices.

Decision: For this delivery cycle, prototype a handheld device for cleaners to transmit estimate and customer sign-off of a completed job.

CSR able to work off-site

Benefits: Providing a virtual office environment and supporting tools appeals to CSRs who want flexibility and want to save on travel expenses. SK can save on office space and expenses.

Risks: SK staff are relatively new, turnover is high. Many CSRs need oversight during their first few months on the job, which would be difficult to provide if they work virtually.

Decision: For this delivery cycle, the product will be used by CSRs in the SK office.

Results of the Environment's Physical Properties Analysis

High-value options that will be included in this delivery cycle are noted with a star (*).

Users	Locations	Physical Conditions	Composition	Access Mode
Cleaner	Off-site, outside & inside customer's property*	Primarily outside, under variable weather conditions.*	Handheld mobile device. Must fit in one hand, weight not to exceed 4 lbs. Four-hour battery life.*	Touchscreen, pen, vibrate, auditory confirmation with max 105 decibels, average 80 decibels*
	SK Office	No dedicated space	Laptop	
	Supply warehouse	No temperature control	Laptop	
	Vehicle	Cramped	Laptop	

continued on next page

CSR	Off-site	Variable networked space	Laptop	
	SK office*	Noisy, shared, congested office space*	Desktop*	Keyboard* Mouse*
Inventory Manager	Supply warehouse	No temperature control	Laptop. Handheld mobile device.	
Sales Manager	SK office	Noisy, congested office space	Laptop	Keyboard Mouse
	Vehicle	Off-site	Mobile device	Touchscreen

2. Technology platform options

2.a. Explore the technology platform options.

? What software—the infrastructure plumbing—will be used to develop, deploy, and operate the product? Options include application programing interfaces, backup and error recovery, browsers, change control, configuration management, data storage, database management, distributed communications, exception handling, installation, libraries, memory, messaging, middleware, networks and distribution services, operating systems, scheduling, security.

? What hardware—physical equipment, media, and devices—will be used to develop, deploy, and operate the product? Options include CPU, disk space, hubs, input-output processers and devices, memory, power supply, routers, switches, and other machines that contain software, firmware, or other hardware components.

? What standards and protocols will be used for messaging, networking, and development languages?

Software	AnxiousAntiVirus BigBox Relational Database ElephantOpenSourceDataStorage Emerald 2.1Developer Language greatBrowser3.2 and above iAmBrowser7.2 and above BigSoft Operating System Penguin Operating System Upstart Operating System Tea Leaves API Tomato Testing Tool
Hardware	Cassidy3500Router ConnectEmPrintHTK Servers Farmer54Application Servers FastSwitch 73 NiceMedia91 Disk Drives
Standards	DistributedDataStandard 4.3 Open Connection Network Protocol Telecom IP

2.b. Evaluate the technology platform options by referencing the goals, objectives, and value considerations.

Which data storage mechanism (database) will be used?

Database options

BigBox Relational Database

Benefit: This database is installed and stable.

Risks: License contract is expiring in three months; new pricing is rumored to be the same or slightly higher. Harder to find engineers with BigBox-specific SQL skills.

ElephantOpenSourceDataStorage

Benefit: This distributed data software is expected to reduce storage cost and ease porting data to distributed locations. This could position SK for franchising and international markets.

Risks: Untrained technical staff for development and maintenance

Some infrequent stability issues are reported.

Potential delays due to mapping and transporting data to new storage mechanism.

Decision: For this delivery cycle, use the ElephantOpenSourceDataStorage

Don't Forget

Exploring Environments

Look for environment options in:

- Existing architecture and infrastructure elements and standards.
- Predefined technology standards. Determine whether you must comply with them or have the flexibility to adjust standards or introduce new ones.
- Consulting with advisers within and outside the organization as you research options for emerging technologies.
- Observation of users interacting with the product to understand their operational environment.

Evaluating Environments

When you're evaluating environments, consider:

Alignment with strategy
- Technical roadmap
- Internal and external hardware and software standards
- Internal and technical infrastructure readiness
- Competitive positioning or differentiation

Usage
- Customer safety
- Physical environment currently in use
- Customer preferences, ergonomics, and aesthetics
- New technologies

Asset utilization
- Reuse of existing software, hardware, and standards
- Ability to install and service the product

Policies and regulations
- Legal costs and expertise to verify standards adherence

Financial impact
- Total cost of ownership: cost to acquire, license, install, train, maintain, operate, and upgrade any changes to your operational or development environment.

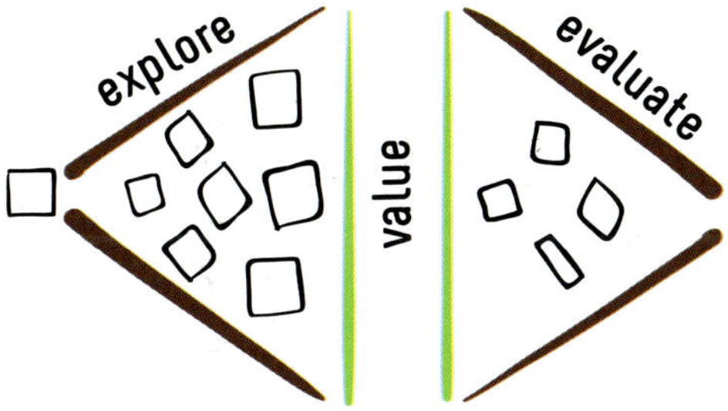

Quality Attribute

1. Quality attribute options

1.a. Explore options for the current view of the product.

? Which quality attributes are needed to support the User, Interface, Action, Data, and Control Dimension?

? Does the quality attribute apply locally to one or a subset of actions, interfaces, controls, etc., or does it apply across all dimensions (that is, is it *cross-cutting)?*

? Will the quality attribute be applied universally? Or will it be specific to:
   Business location (geographical boundary)
   Organizational boundary

? Who is authorized to specify the quality attribute (e.g., authorized person, governing body)?

List the quality attribute options.

Availability: The SK scheduling application will be available 95% of the time Monday through Friday from 8:00 a.m. to 5:00 p.m. Eastern time. The SK scheduling application will be available 95% of the time Saturday 8:00 a.m. to 2 p.m. Eastern time.

Installability: An untrained user will be able to install upgrades to the SK application within 10 minutes without accessing any printed documentation.

Performance: The calculated price for requested services shall be displayed within two seconds of completing entry of the service type and count.

Scalability: SK scheduling functionality will be capable of supporting 15 franchises in the next two calendar years.

Security: All query and reporting functions shall comply with security and data privacy requirements SecPiv 301.2.

1.b. Evaluate options by referencing the goals, objectives, and value considerations.

Availability: The SK scheduling application will be available 95% of the time Monday through Friday from 8:00 a.m. to 5:00p.m. Eastern time. The SK scheduling application will be available 95% of the time Saturday 8:00 a.m. to 2 p.m. Eastern time.

Benefit: CSRs' productivity diminishes rapidly when the system is down and they have to revert to paper scheduling, resulting in delays, rework, and errors.

Decision: Meet minimum availability level, per service level agreement.

Installability: An untrained user will be able to install upgrades to the SK application within 10 minutes without accessing any printed documentation.

Benefits: Quick and easy installs are critical for franchise expansion. Addressing the future needs for franchising during this delivery cycle will reduce the need for significant changes when franchising is launched (e.g., reduce technical debt).

Risks: Building in scalability will slow down delivery of the current delivery cycle's solution. Decision on franchise expansion has not been made.

Decision: Do not consider installability in the current delivery cycle's development.

Performance: The calculated price for requested services will be displayed within two seconds of entering each service type and count.

Benefit: Quick and efficient scheduling improves customer and CSR satisfaction.

Risk: Response time for high volumes or peak times has not been tested; service level agreement prescribes three seconds.

Decision: Meet service level agreement response time level of a maximum of three seconds for this delivery cycle. For subsequent delivery cycles, test the performance impact of high-volume requests.

Scalability: SK scheduling functionality will be capable of supporting 15 franchises in the next two calendar years.

Benefit: Addressing the future needs for franchising during this delivery cycle will reduce the need for significant changes when franchising is launched (e.g., reduce technical debt).

Risks: Building in scalability will slow down completion of the current delivery cycle's solution. Decision on franchise expansion has not been made.

Decision: Do not factor in scaling for franchise expansion in the current delivery cycle's development.

Security: A customer's preferred payment details will be protected from unauthorized access.

Benefit: Many customers want the convenience of not having to reenter their preferred payment method, but they need assurance that the data will be secure.

Risk: SK could be fined (depending on jurisdiction) if unauthorized access of customer payment data occurs. SK risks adverse publicity if data is accessed inappropriately.

Decision: Too complex to build security infrastructure in this delivery cycle. Do not store customer's preferred payment method data.

Results of Quality Attribute Dimension Analysis

High-value options that will be included in this delivery cycle are noted with a star (*).

Quality Attribute Type	Quality Attribute Options	Metric Options
Availability*	The SK scheduling application will be available 95% of the time Monday through Friday from 8:00 a.m. to 5:00 p.m. Eastern time. The SK scheduling application will be available Saturday 8:00 a.m. to 2 p.m. Eastern time.*	Planguage
Installability	An untrained user will be able to install upgrades to the SK application within 10 minutes without accessing any printed documentation.	
Performance*	The calculated price for requested services shall be displayed within three seconds of entering each service type and count.*	Quality Attribute Scenario
Scalability	The SK scheduling functionality will be capable of supporting 15 franchises in the next two calendar years.	
Security	A customer's preferred payment details will be protected from unauthorized access	

Don't Forget

Exploring Quality Attributes

- Look for *operational quality attribute* options for high-value users, interfaces, actions, and data options.
- Look for *development quality attribute* options for high-value hardware and software options.
- Create a prototype to explore operational and development quality attributes.

  Prototype
- Observe users interacting with the prototype or the deployed product to learn about their expectations and tolerance levels for operational properties, e.g., availability, performance, reliability, and usability.
- To aid in exploring quality attribute options for interfaces, sketch a context diagram. There may be unique properties that apply to specific interfaces, e.g., performance, usability, security, availability, and safety.

  Context Diagram
- Explore quality attributes specific to product documentation, such as user manuals, help guides, and installation notes.
- Consider whether a quality attribute is cross-cutting (applies to all or a subset of the product's options) or is unique to one option. Example: providing security for specific data.

Writing Quality Attributes

Writing formats:

- Narrative story, "As a Security Monitor, I need privacy data to be protected, so…"
- Keyword-driven language:

  Planguage, Quality Attribute Scenario
- Write measurable, testable properties. Use ranges to identify acceptable boundaries.

Evaluating Quality Attributes

When you're evaluating quality attribute options, consider:

Planning and delivery

- Incremental delivery of more rigorous levels of quality attributes. For example, initially deliver "less than 4-second response time," in subsequent delivery cycles "less than 2-second response time."
- Focusing a release (or iteration) on a quality attribute theme. For example, "High Volume Search," "Scale for Franchising," or "Localization for Non-U.S. Deployment."
- Including product-differentiating quality attributes on your product roadmap.
- There is a cumulative nature to quality attributes. Once you implement a quality attribute, it will need to be tested and implemented for subsequent delivery cycles.

Alignment with strategy

- Technical roadmap
- Internal and external standards, e.g., usability, security, accessibility
- Ability to support the desired level within the current environment
- Competitive positioning or differentiation

Usage

- Criticality of customer experience (usability) for product success
- Customer preferences, ergonomics, and aesthetics

Asset utilization

- Reuse of existing hardware and software components to accomplish desired quality attributes

Financial implications

- Cost for acquiring, licensing, or upgrading hardware and software to deliver desired levels of quality attributes
- Cumulative testing costs (e.g., when new functionality is added, test new and existing functionality)

Focus Questions for the Structured Conversation

To explore the product options for the current and future product, you can use focus questions.

	Users	Interfaces	Actions	Data	Controls	Environment	Quality Attributes
Users		How will the user interface with the product?	Will the user's goal be supported by an action? Who will initiate an action?	What data will the user need?	Will the user be constrained by a control?	Where will the user be when interacting with the product? What is the environment like?	Will the user need specific quality attributes when using the product?
Interfaces	Who (human, other systems) will be using the interface to interact with the product?		Will an inbound interface trigger an action? Will an outbound interface be generated by an action?	Will the product's input and output data be traced to one or more interfaces?	Will the interface enforce a control?	Where will interfaces be accessed? How will interfaces be accessed?	Will interfaces be qualified by quality attributes?
Actions	What action will the user initiate?	Will the action need an interface?		What actions will create, read, update, and delete data? What actions will transition a data entity from one state to another?	Will the action enforce a control?	Will the action take place in certain physical locations? Will the action take place on certain technical platforms?	Will actions be qualified by quality attributes?

Data	What data will the user access?	What data will be communicated through interfaces?	What data will actions create, read, update, and delete?		Will the data be constrained by controls?	Where will the data be located? Will the data conform to certain data standards for storage, network access, and concurrency?	Will the data be qualified by specific quality attributes?
Controls	What controls will be specific to a user?	Will a control be enforced in an interface?	What controls will an action enforce?	Will a control be specific to a data entity or attribute?		Will the control's jurisdiction and enforcement levels be specific to a location? Will controls be stored and enforced by a technical platform?	Will controls be qualified by specific quality attributes?
Environments	What will be the physical locations where users will access the product?	What physical access mechanisms will be used to interface with the product?	Where will the actions take place? What tecnology platform will be used to operate system actions?	What technology platforms will be used to access, store, distribute, back up, and recover the data? What standards for data will be used?	Will a location require certain controls? Will there be a technical platform to store and enforce controls?		Will controls be qualified by specific quality attributes?
Quality Attributes	Will there be quality attributes specific to users?	What quality attributes will qualify the interfaces?	Will there be quality attributes specific to one or more actions?	Will there be quality attributes for the data?	Will quality attributes be applied to controls?	Will the quality attributes be supported by the technology platform?	

Focus Questions for the Structured Conversation

Section 5

ADAPT

ADAPTING YOUR PRACTICES

Virtually every project, product, and situation is unique, and teams need to make major or minor adaptations in their practices to accommodate their situation. The beauty of Agile/Lean is that it's highly adaptable. (If you're unfamiliar with Agile delivery, see our online references and recommended readings at www.DiscoverToDeliver.com)

In this section, you'll find a set of high-level suggestions for ways to adapt your planning and analysis practices.

- Adapting your structured conversation
- Adapting to harmonize with your delivery method
- Adapting to acquire and integrate commercial software
- Adapting your documentation practices
- Adapting your process when you're developing regulated products

Adapting Your Structured Conversation

In your structured conversations, your aim is to maximize quality and minimize your time investment. A little planning will help. Regardless of your project or product, here are general steps that will help you have productive conversations.

1. Identify your planning view.
2. Select your starting product dimension.
3. Identify your navigation path.
4. Select tools and techniques to supplement your conversation.
5. Conduct retrospectives on your process and product, and adjust accordingly.

1. Identify your planning view.

Context counts—a lot. Know the scope of your time horizon: Big-View, Pre-View, or Now-View. Perhaps it's a combination, such as combined release and iteration planning (Pre-View and Now-View) or combined product roadmapping and release planning (Big-View and Pre-View).

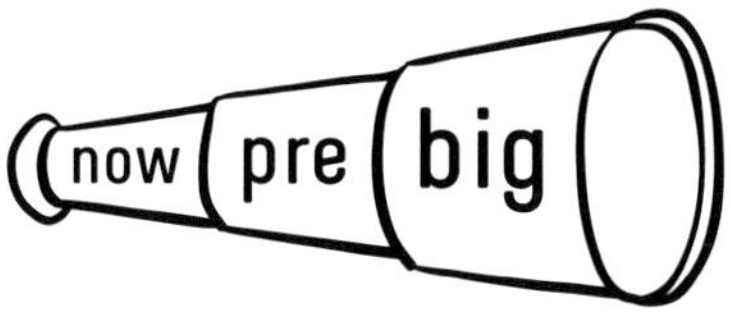

When might you combine views? Perhaps you're starting a new development effort. Or you've just completed a release of the product and are embarking on your next release planning. You might combine views when the partners recognize they need to reach a shared understanding of the vision and product.

2. Select your starting product dimension.

See examples in "Leading with…" (Section 3, The Structured Conversation).

As you converse, be prepared to move back and forth across dimensions. Supplement your conversations with analysis models and examples, making the artifacts visible on your Options board.

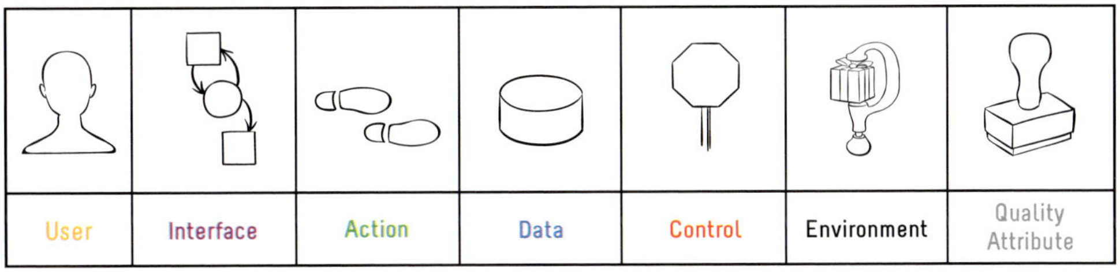

The sequence and granularity of your exploration may vary depending on the planning view. For example, you might explore features during Big-View product roadmapping conversations, or stories during Now-View conversations.

3. Identify your navigation path.

You can explore product options by navigating top-down, bottom-up, or middle-out. For example, you might begin with the Pre-View and navigate to the Now-View in a single conversation, or focus on the Now-View and then navigate to the Pre-View, and so on.

4. Select tools and techniques to supplement your conversation.

Expand your conversation toolkit and enrich your structured conversations by using tools and techniques that supplement your conversations. You'll find a sample set of these tools and techniques in Section 6.

5. Conduct retrospectives on your process and product, and adjust accordingly.

Product discovery and delivery is complicated (Appelo, 2012). Conduct retrospectives to obtain feedback on your conversation process and products. Identify specific actions you can take to adjust your structured conversations and improve on them.

Structured Conversation Levers: Scope, Frequency, and Formality

You can adjust various levers to support your structured conversations.

Scope refers to the breadth of product needs you're discussing.

- Large Scope: Big-View; Big-View and Pre-View; large product or portfolio of products
- Small Scope: Now-View; single product

Frequency refers to how often your conversations occur.

- Frequent: Continually conversing (daily, hourly, multiple times per day or week)
- Infrequent: Conversing periodically (every two weeks, once per month, at quarter end)

Formality refers to the amount of preparation you do.

- Formal: Schedule people and rooms days or weeks in advance; use neutral, skilled facilitator; craft draft analysis models, examples, and other exploration tools; define detailed agenda; prepare posters, markers, walls. Conduct "show and tell" sharing sessions with higher-level partners afterward. Such structured conversations tend to take hours (versus minutes).
- Informal: Slide a chair over to a nearby partner and start a conversation; use online tools to instant message; move to a readily available room with little notice.

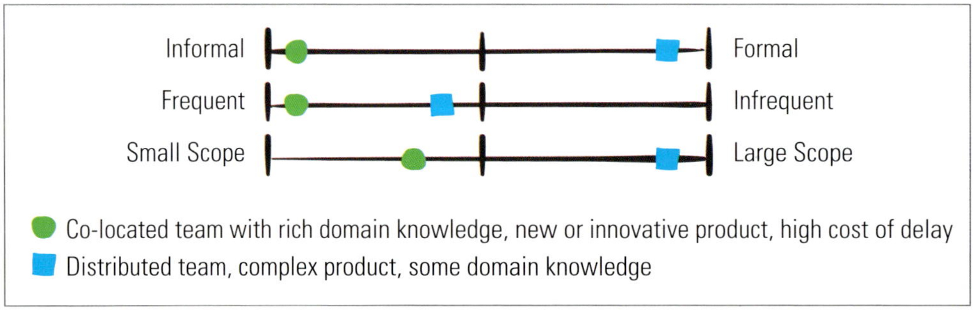

Adapting Your Structured Conversation

Factors to Consider When Adapting Your Structured Conversation

Product Factors	Considerations
Product complexity	Complex products may benefit from frequent conversations.
Stability of product needs	With volatile product needs, hold frequent conversations. Narrow the scope of these conversations.
Risk of diminished value	Frequent, broad conversations help to clarify value and build trust.

Team Factors	Considerations
Delivery team domain expertise	Frequent conversations increase domain knowledge.
Number of partners	Larger teams may need more formal conversations.
Partner risks	A new team, new team members, people unfamiliar with product domain, external technical partners may benefit from frequent conversations.
Physical proximity of partners	Co-located teams may have more frequent, informal, small-scope conversations.
Strength of the partner relationship	You can have more infrequent and informal conversations with stronger, trusting partnerships and a shared understanding of product needs.

Adapting to Harmonize with Your Delivery Method

The discovery practices in this book are helpful no matter which delivery method you are using: traditional (waterfall), timebox (Scrum), or flow (Kanban). Adapt your structured conversations based on your delivery method.

Traditional teams typically converse about all product needs in a single sweep, essentially collapsing the Pre-View and the Now-View. Subsequent conversations about product needs occur on demand when questions arise or the partners recognize that requirements need to change or the project scope needs to be altered.

On Agile teams, structured conversations occur multiple times, as the team completes a delivery cycle and returns to discover product needs for the next planning cycle. This happens for each planning view.

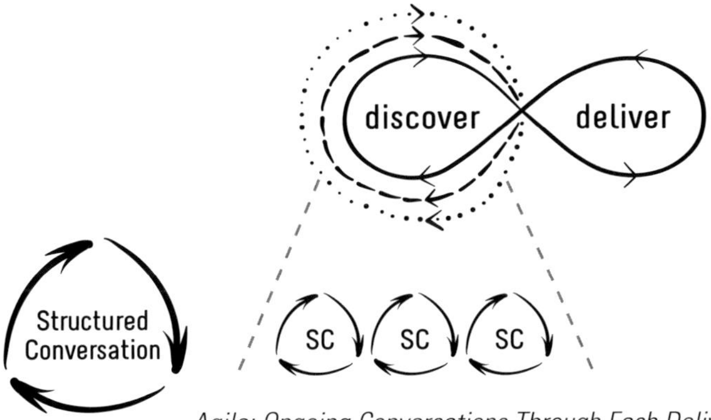

Agile: Ongoing Conversations Through Each Delivery

For any delivery method, Big-View conversations are scheduled around planning cycles, project or program start-up (charter), or the need for a product roadmap. Pre-View structured conversations have a different cadence than those in the Now-view.

Delivery Method	Triggers for Structured Conversation	
	Pre-View	Now-View
Traditional	Scheduled: • End of major milestone (requirements, design, etc.) • Project or program charter approved • Funding approval • Quarterly planning cycle	Scheduled: Requirements phase On demand: When questions arise during any subsequent phase (e.g., design, test)
Timebox	Scheduled: End of a release and release retrospective (time to conduct release planning)	Scheduled: • One or more times before iteration planning (to refine, estimate, and plan items for upcoming iterations) • Iteration planning (to further refine, estimate, and plan items for the current iteration) On demand: Whenever a work item (e.g., story) is started Continual: When questions arise about a work item during the iteration
Flow	Scheduled: End of a release and release retrospective (to conduct release planning)	On demand: When queue opens to begin work on a backlog (queue) item Continual: When questions arise about a work item during development

Triggers for Structured Conversations

Structured Conversations for Traditional Delivery

Teams using a traditional delivery approach have conversations that encompass a wide scope of product needs. The conversations take place during the project's requirements or analysis phase and conclude with formal documents representing a given batch of product needs.

Structured Conversations for Timebox Delivery

Delivery teams using a timebox delivery approach have conversations to plan and prepare product needs for the next iteration, as well as one to three subsequent iterations. Now-View structured conversations on agile teams are focused on small sets of product needs that can be delivered in hours, days, or weeks. The goals of these short preparation sessions (typically one to three hours) are to:

- Identify which product needs are likely to be delivered in upcoming iterations. The conversations can be scheduled (e.g., twice a week) or requested on demand.
- Learn about requirements for the current iteration by making them ready for testing and development.

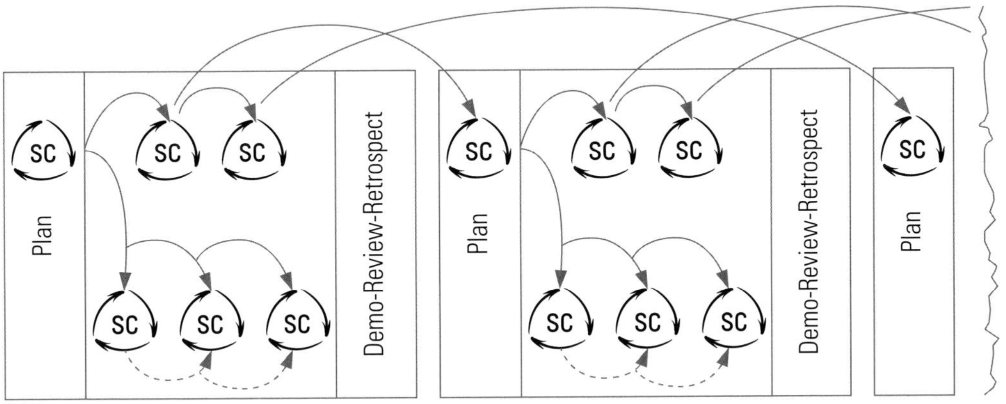

Timebox Structured Conversations: Feed Current & Upcoming Iterations

Structured Conversations for Flow Delivery

If you're using a *flow delivery* approach, such as Kanban, you can expect your structured conversations to happen continually. Conversations are triggered when work-in-progress limits permit you to pull product needs—stories, features, or MMFs—from the input queue (product backlog) into the analysis queue.

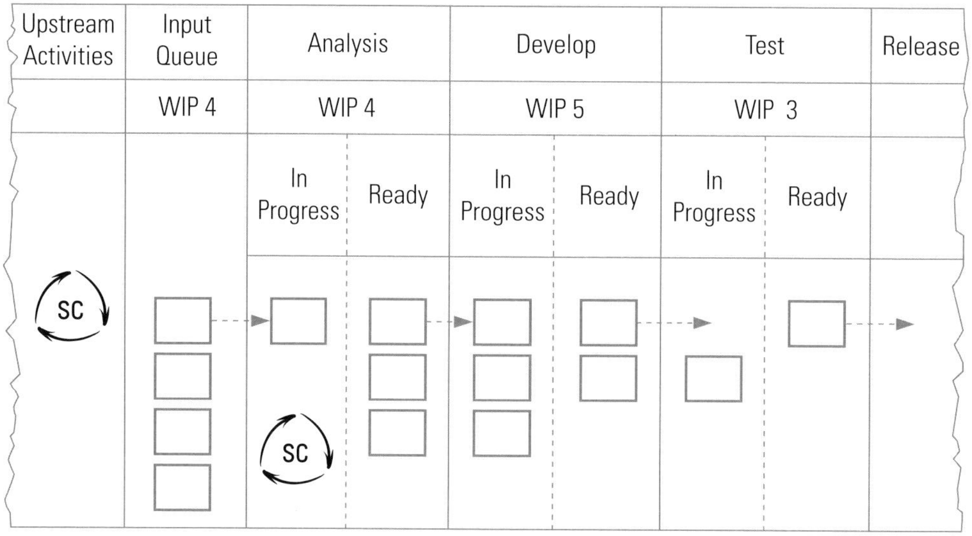

Flow Delivery: Continuous Structured Conversations

Upstream activities, such as release planning or product roadmapping, feed the input queue. The team may need to slice large product needs into smaller, similarly sized items during their structured conversations. Kanban teams can establish guaranteed service levels for developing these sliced items—for example, a two- to four-day cycle time.

As shown in the example that follows, you might slice a large item, such as a feature, into three like-sized items. One is valued high for delivery. That item will flow through development and testing and will be assembled for final testing and release.

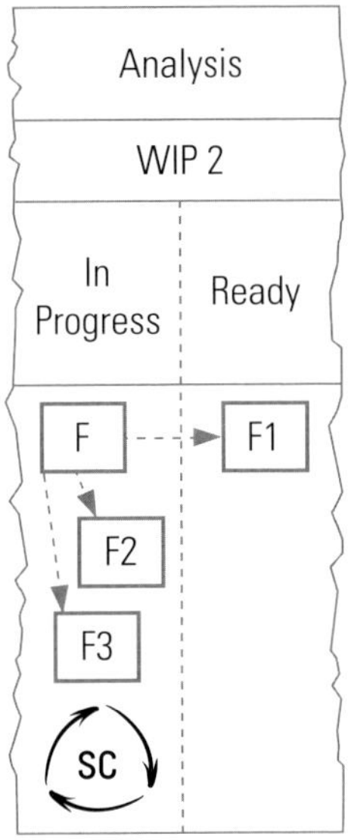

Flow Delivery: Using the Structured Conversation to Slice Large Product Needs

Queue size is a leading indicator of cycle time problems (Anderson, 2010, and Reinersten, 2009). For this reason, teams using Kanban can reduce cycle times and speed delivery by having a small queue of product needs—at each view. A shorter queue ensures that high-value candidate solutions are delivered sooner.

Ready-for-Development Checklist

We recommend that Agile teams, no matter what delivery method they use, agree on a criteria checklist that specifies a requirement as ready to be developed and tested (timebox) or ready to pull into the development lane (flow).

Adapting to Acquire and Integrate Commercial Software

The discovery practices in this book are helpful when you select, purchase, and implement commercial software products. They can also aid during delivery, when the emphasis is on configuration, integration, and testing.

> **By Any Other Name**
> There are numerous names for commercial software that is produced for sale and integrated into your portfolio of software applications. Names include commercially available off-the-shelf (COTS) software, commercial software packages, package acquisition, packaged software, payware, and software packages.

When you're exploring options for purchasing a commercial software product, structure your questions along the 7 Product Dimensions.

- User: Who will use the product (people, other products, systems)?
- Interface: What interfaces are needed? What is the status of these interfaces (new; existing, use as is; existing, change or replace)? What are the interface types?
- Action: What actions must the product provide?
- Data: What data must the product create and store? What format is it in? How granular is it? Can the product's data be customized or configured? What data must the product access? What are the sources of that data?
- Control: What business rules must the product enforce? Can the commercial software's rules be customized or configured? Can (or should) your organization change policies and business rules to match those in the product?
- Environment: On what technical platform must the commercial software run? To what development standards must the product conform?
- Quality attribute: What quality attributes must your product support, and at what level? For example, what are specific acceptance criteria for performance, throughput, security, reliability, and usability?

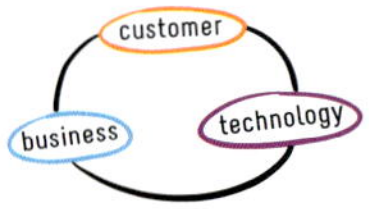

A commercial software provider (or vendor) is both a business and a technology partner.

The commercial software provider may have distinct value considerations. For example, as a business partner, your provider may value increasing its revenue, enhancing brand recognition for its product, and making minimal changes to its product. As a technology partner, a provider may—or may not—prefer that you install its product only on the technical platforms it currently supports. Be sure you understand both sets of values. They are useful during your final selection and negotiation process and in forming a transparent, trusting partnership.

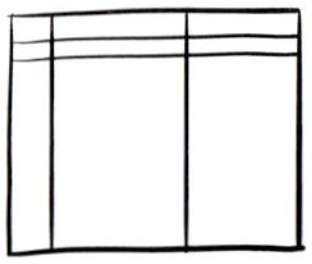

Implementing a commercial software product creates a dependency on your provider, thereby heightening project risk. At all planning views, collaborate to identify risks, define risk detection indicators, and agree on mitigation actions. Your implementation plan is tightly coupled to your provider's plan. We recommend conducting collaborative product roadmapping and release planning workshops to transparently build and revise plans.

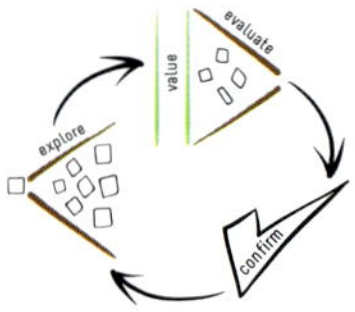

Acquiring commercial software, versus building your own, does not change the fact that you need to discover product needs and conduct structured conversations to explore, evaluate, and confirm the product.

In addition to understanding your specific product needs, explore potential vendors' product documentation—for example, feature-benefit documents, customer testimonials, product comparison worksheets, demonstrations, and the like. Combine document analysis with other exploration techniques such as contextual inquiry and facilitated workshops. By combining a variety of discovery techniques, you uncover product differentiators that might not be part of a commercial product.

When you're selecting useful analysis models for your structured conversations, consider:

- Your glossary is essential for establishing a shared understanding of domain terms not only within your organization but also with your potential provider.
- Your data model or data dictionary can clarify the relevant data and support data integration and migration during delivery.
- Stories, scenarios, data examples, and *acceptance criteria lists* are useful to discover product needs, to guide product demonstrations (when you compare competing products), to guide configuration decisions, and to migrate data and conduct testing during delivery.

Adapting Your Documentation Practices

The main purpose of product or process documentation is communication. Consider your partners as documentation consumers. When you weigh how much to invest in discovering and delivering product documentation, assess the partners' value considerations.

Product Documentation

Product documentation conveys information about the product and is an asset used to sell, use, and service the product and to provide evidence for regulatory compliance.

The partners use various kinds of documentation:

- Customer partners: user guides; help and job aids; training; installation and update guides; licensing agreements; release notes; marketing collateral (sales sheets, product data sheets and white papers, features and benefits, sales presentations, product demonstrations, product comparisons); external product roadmaps
- Business partners: regulatory documents; product plans; competitive analyses
- Technology partners: requirements and design documents used to maintain the product; service level agreements; reports such as customer complaints and bug reports used to enhance and service the product

Process Documentation

Process documentation captures work-in-progress (WIP) or handovers to partners involved in discovery and delivery.

WIP documentation helps you to remember what you're exploring (posters, examples, analysis models, prototypes), evaluating (value considerations), and confirming (acceptance criteria). WIP documentation also includes assets (task or workflow boards, project dashboards, release plans) that the team and management use to monitor and track discovery and delivery.

Handover information is used by business and technology partners to share information. Examples include requirements, design, and test documents; error logs; data about special processing; and test results. Handover documentation is not a substitute for the exploration work that goes into creating it. In fact, it may introduce inefficiencies in product delivery (Reinersten, 2009, and Poppendieck & Poppendieck, 2009).

You can use document templates for organizing handover information (marketing documents, requirements documents, software requirements specifications). Well-designed templates can increase usability (Rüping, 2003). Consider how you might repurpose process documentation as product documentation for regulatory agencies.

Volume and Value

More does not mean better. In fact, having more documentation can decrease its usability and therefore reduce its value to consumers.

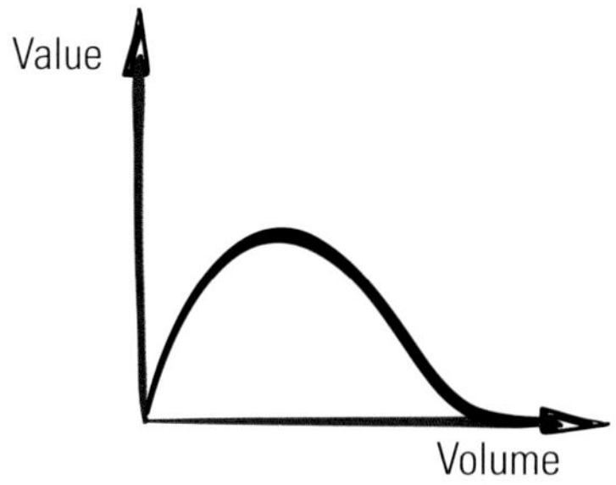

Potential Nonlinear Relationship between Documentation's Volume and Value

In general, product documentation is more valuable than process documentation and more costly to create and maintain.

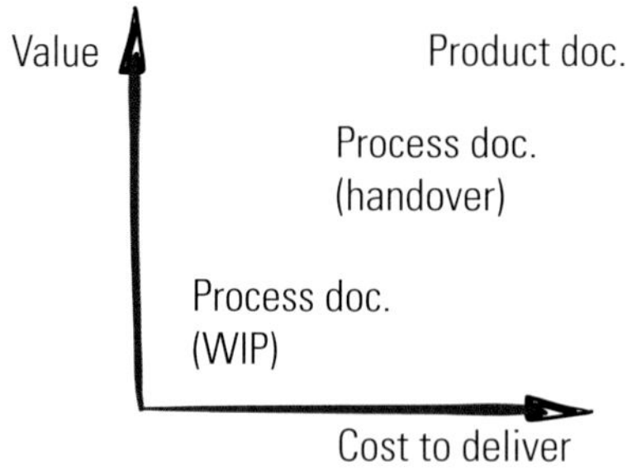

Value & Cost to Deliver Product & Process Documentation

Documentation Considerations

Product Documentation	Process Documentation	Both
• Consider all 7 Product Dimensions to explore needs. • Specify testable acceptance criteria. • Consider product documentation as part of acceptance criteria for candidate solutions.	• For a regulated product, you may need to document your verification and validation processes.	• Assess usefulness early by creating prototypes. • Conduct retrospectives on usefulness.

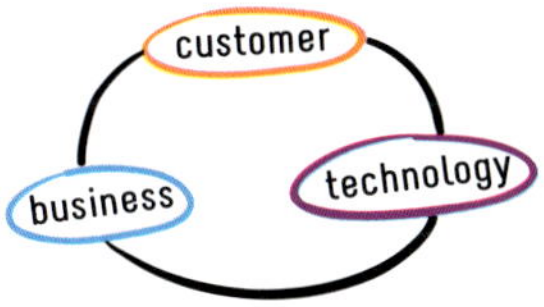

Product Documentation	Process Documentation	Both
• Identify users and their usability needs. • Engage external customers and advisers (potential customers, regulatory advisers, sales and marketing, auditors, legal experts) in discovering and confirming product documentation.	• Engage partners to explore the minimum necessary and useful WIP and handover documentation.	• Seek early, continual feedback on quality.

value

Product Documentation	Process Documentation	Both
• Elicit customer and business partner value considerations. • Define acceptance criteria based on these values.	• Identify technology partner value considerations, and adjust formality and precision.	• Have partners review early prototype documents; adjust formality and precision to minimize waste and maximize value.

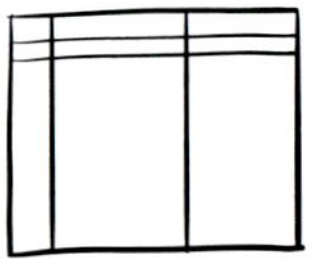

Both Product and Process Documentation
• Use plans (product roadmaps, release plans, iteration plans, Kanban or workflow boards) at all views to communicate.

Product Documentation	Process Documentation
• Use analysis models and examples in user manuals, training guides, support documents, and marketing collateral.	• Use output from your structured conversations as your WIP documentation. • Decide what will be retained, formalized, and further developed. • Your Options board and photos of posters are a form of WIP documentation.

Documentation Levers: Formality, Precision, and Stability

You can adjust the formality, precision, and stability of documentation.

Formality

Formality refers to the degree of adherence to standards, the automation used to create documentation, and the ceremony attached to it.

- Informal: Uses nonstandard formats; uses few electronic tools; may be photographs, paper and posters, or online tools.
- Formal: Uses predefined templates; generated and tracked with electronic tools; contains sign-off and approval signatures; includes traceability matrices; consumed by internal and external parties (customers, business partners, regulatory agencies); retained for many years; expensive to discover and deliver.

Precision

Precision refers to the degree of detail and accuracy.

- Imprecise: Nonstandard contents, coarse-grained, abstract.
- More precise: Contains details about the 7 Product Dimensions or examples; provides verification for regulatory agencies.

Stability

Stability refers to how often documentation changes.

- Less stable: Frequently updated (daily or weekly); is temporarily accurate, short-lived, and seldom retained beyond delivery cycle.
- More stable: Periodically updated; content tends to be wide and shallow.

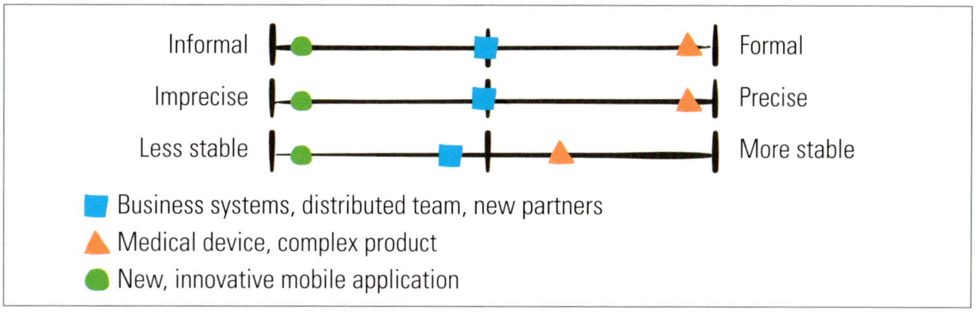

Adapting Your Documentation for Different Products

Factors to Consider When Adapting Your Documentation

Product Factors	Considerations
Commercial product	• Requires formal and precise documentation. • Documentation is an asset—study users and usability needs.
Product complexity	• Complex products benefit from precision and stability.
Regulatory product	• Documentation is crucial for product success. • Traceability is useful for verification. • Formal, precise documentation is typically warranted. • Precise and updated WIP documentation can mitigate risks of noncompliance.

Team Factors	Considerations
Delivery team domain expertise	• When the delivery team has rich domain knowledge, they may not need highly precise process documents.
Number of product partners	• Larger teams may need more process documentation to aid communication.
Partner risks	• With new or changing partners; an unfamiliar product or domain; and external technical partners or technology risks, you need formal, precise, and stable process documents to mitigate risks.
Physical proximity of partners	• When product partners are nearby, documents may be less formal and precise. • Co-located teams can use an Options board for WIP documents.
Strength of the partner relationship	• When the partners have a trusting relationship, you can use fewer handover documents.

Adapting Your Process When You're Developing Regulated Products

When your product must comply with regulations, you need to provide evidence that it delivers its capabilities in a manner that complies with the regulations. You may need to discover and deliver additional product capabilities outside the needs of your users. Typically you need capabilities such as audit, authentication, security, and data capture and storage. You also may need to precisely and formally document your product development and change management processes.

The cost of noncompliance may include fines (resulting in lost revenue), public exposure (loss of reputation, often resulting in lost investment, reduced revenue, and decreased company valuation), or legal action (loss of revenue or even the entire organization).

Regulated (or *high-assurance)* products may protect against loss of life, health, money, and a safe environment. Domains include pharmaceuticals, healthcare, medical devices, food and food industries, financial services, utilities, gaming, defense, commercial and military aeronautics, transportation, and the like.

Verify and Validate

Verification and validation are crucial issues. You may need to demonstrate that the product was developed using a defined process, that the process was followed (verification) and that the process produced a product of a specified quality (validation).

A useful analogy for verification and validation is management and leadership:

- Managers make sure you do things correctly (verification).
- Leaders make sure you do the right things (validation).

Regulations often do not prescribe how to implement verification and validation. In practice, you comply with verification by tracing high-level product needs (such as features listed in a document) to precise artifacts used to develop, test, and implement the feature. You demonstrate validation by specifying high-level product needs, conducting demonstrations, inspections, and reviews, building *operational prototypes*, and conducting *acceptance tests*.

It is a misconception that you can't use Agile methods to build regulated products. In practice, for regulated products you adapt your processes for exploring, evaluating, and confirming product needs by using greater formality, precision, and ceremony to manage change control, implement requirements traceability, and document development practices.

If you're building a regulated product, be attentive to specific regulatory needs for each of the 7 Product Dimensions. Some examples:

- User: Who has access to the product? Who audits and reviews for compliance?
- Interface: Do you need additional security?
- Action: What audit actions are needed? Do you need specific authentication actions to prevent use of the product in dangerous ways?
- Data: What are the allowable threshold levels for safety-critical data? For audit data? For traceability?
- Control: Do specific regulations or policies apply?
- Environment: Are there physical constraints that impact safety and reliability?
- Quality attribute: Do you need to provide evidence of conformance to regulations regarding usability? Ability to find crucial and sensitive answers? Ability of auditors to find answers to conformance questions?

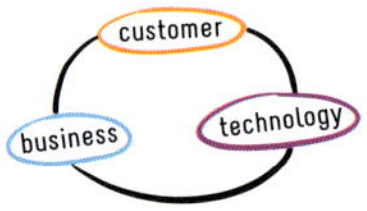

Explicitly identify business and customer partners who have expertise on regulations. Examples include external auditors and examiners (customers of your compliance documentation) and people from your business units such as legal, regulatory and compliance, audit, and quality assurance. They provide ongoing validation feedback.

If you don't have direct access to external regulators, engage internal regulatory experts as surrogates. They can help you craft your documentation (content and degree of precision), serve as inspectors, and confirm you're supplying adequate evidence of product and process compliance.

value

Be sure to explicitly explore the partners' value considerations early in planning. Some examples:

- Customer partners' value considerations: Medical device product customers value *safety*, *efficiency*, reliability, performance, and usability. Financial product customers value protecting revenue and security, among other things.
- Business partners' value considerations: Protecting revenue and mitigating risks associated with noncompliance.
- Technology partners' value considerations: Reusing components, conducting rigorous tests, and minimizing the overhead associated with documentation.

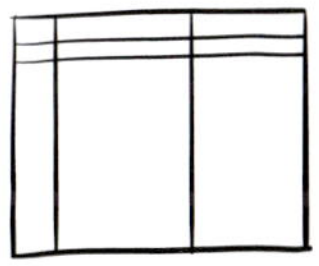

Plan to replan, and focus on reducing risk. Risks are amplified when your product includes embedded software and hardware components. Some guidelines:

- Identify and specify your development process, document it, and put the process itself under change control. Be sure all partners collaborate in creating, managing, and continually reviewing the process.
- Incorporate compliance requirements, code, tests, and document inspections and reviews into all delivery cycles. Be selective about what to inspect and review. Use inspections and reviews for high-risk items.
- Use retrospectives in each delivery cycle to assess risks and evaluate the health of your verification and validation practices and outcomes. Adjust them as needed.
- Use early delivery cycles to prototype and test your requirements traceability matrices in order to gain experience in inspections and reviews. Tune these practices to keep them as lightweight as possible, but sufficient for you to be in compliance.
- Conduct Big-View planning as early as possible, and deliver a document containing your high-level product needs (such as a product or marketing requirements document) to serve as a baseline for your traceability matrices.
- Use your early Pre-View delivery cycles to deliver high-risk, high-value components and to confirm your verification (tracing) practices and product needs (validation). This practice is vital to protect your investment in people, time, and money. Use theme names that reflect these delivery cycles' risk-reduction goals.

- Use Pre-View delivery cycles to integrate all delivery components, both hardware and software. To streamline system and integration testing and reduce the cost and delays of manual testing, continually increase your automated testing practices. Use your Pre-View delivery cycles to adjust to changes in hardware, review safety issues, and reduce overall technology risks.

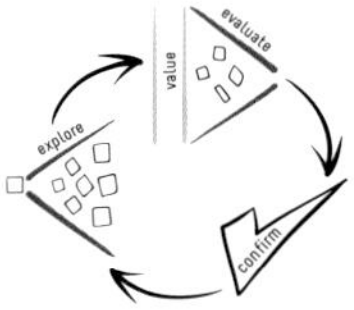

Structured conversations for regulated products need formal, frequent, and precise confirmation. Engage regulatory advisers to help you identify how to confirm your candidate solutions. You need precise acceptance criteria for Pre-View and Now-View work, and you need to know how you will test (verify) the product and confirm that it is valid. Consider these practices:

- Test your product documentation early to be sure it meets regulatory needs.
- Formalize your conversations as you explore and evaluate product options.
- Use demos, prototypes, traceability matrices, and videotaped (or otherwise recorded) manual testing.
- Document requirements with mini-specifications, not a mega-specification. Rather than build your specs in one fell swoop, build multiple, smaller specs incrementally as you move through your Pre-View or Now-View delivery cycles.
- Increase the value and usability of your documentation by replacing, or supplementing, the classic "system shall" format with data models, state diagrams, context diagrams, dependency graphs, and so on.

Documentation as a Product

Documentation of both product and process is an important part of your overall product, so it's vital to engage consumers of the documentation in designing the form and format.

Process documentation includes your product development process and processes for change control, requirements management, configuration management, and sign-off. Some regulations may involve delivering test plans, unit test scripts, and system test scripts. Identify who, what, when, how, and where you will provide evidence you are using those processes. When you treat regulatory documentation as a product, it needs its own acceptance criteria, such as usability, reliability, frequency of production, and the users, data, and controls used to produce it.

Facilitated workshops help partners identify regulatory practices and internal work process policies. If you're using Agile methods, create mini-specifications with precise acceptance criteria for your iterations or releases. Focus on content quality and not document volume to create rich, compliant mini-specifications.

Section 6

TOOLS AND TECHNIQUES

TOOLS & TECHNIQUES

Following is a set of essential tools and techniques you'll find useful for exploring, evaluating, and confirming product needs, as well as for communicating with partners about the product-to-be.

By tools and techniques we mean any model (visual representation), artifact, or activity that helps you to engage in rich structured conversations about product needs. You can use these for analysis as well as planning, and you can use them alone or in combination—whatever works for your team. You'll probably recognize a number of these tools and techniques; they transcend delivery method, product type, and product domain.

continued on next page

Tools & Techniques	Usage	Page
Facilitated Workshop	Structured Conversation	228
Feature, MMF, MVP	Action Dimension	230
Given-When-Then	Confirm	231
Glossary	Data Dimension	232
Interaction Matrix	Evaluate	233
Options Board	Product	234
Persona	User Dimension	235
Planguage	Confirm	236
Plan	Plan	237
Product Vision	Product	240
Prototype	Interface Dimension	241
Quality Attribute Scenario	Confirm	242
Relationship Map	Interface Dimension	243
Scenario	Action Dimension	244
Scenario Z Pattern	Action Dimension	245
State Diagram	Data Dimension	246
Story	Action Dimension	247
Story Map	Action Dimension	248
Use Case	Action Dimension	249
User, User Role, User Role Map	User Dimension	250
Value Stream Map	Action Dimension	251
Value Tools	Value	252

Acceptance Criteria List

An acceptance criteria list is used to identify what to test when you're validating a scenario, story, feature, or candidate solution.

Usefulness

You can use the list at varying levels of granularity (scenario, story, feature, or candidate solution). The list's format is flexible. For a more structured approach, use Given-When-Then (in this Tools & Techniques section).

Examples

Story: Schedule a job

Bullet List Form

- The date and time for requested schedule date is valid.
- Job date and time match customer's requested date and time.
- When there is a match (requested date and time can be scheduled), assign an available cleaner to the job and verify:
  - Job data is stored.
  - Confirmation message is provided to the scheduler with the details shown.
- When there is no match, display a list of closest available dates and times.

Stepwise Form

1. Verify the property is within SK's service area on the requested service date.
2. Verify the requested service time is within SK's standard hours of service provision.
3. Display available cleaners (available for requested date and time).
4. Verify the estimated cost is calculated using pricing for that date of service.
5. Provide confirmation or denial message.
6. Verify the confirmation includes job details (date, time, services, property details, cancellation policy, liability policy).

Business Policy, Business Rule

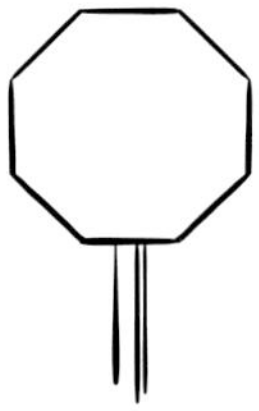

A business policy (or regulation, e.g., the Sarbanes-Oxley Act) defines a principle or regulation that influences the behavior of an organization or a product.

A business rule is a precise textual statement that defines, constrains, or enables the behavior of software, business processes, and data structures.

Usefulness

Defining business polices and rules help you to elicit and validate organization-level decision logic. For estimating and planning, it's essential to understand the complexity of the controls, their sources, jurisdiction, and enforcement levels.

Examples

Policy Group	BP ID	Business Policy
Schedule Job	BP-004	A customer who has not paid for prior services may be prevented from scheduling new services.
	BP-005	A requested service must match a service currently offered by SK.
	BP-006	The customer must agree to be at the property 2 hours prior to job's scheduled time.
	BP-007	A cleaner must not be double-booked.
Discounts	BP-009	A discount may be available depending on the property type and the amount of paid services.
Cancel Job	BP-010	A cancellation may be assessed a cancellation fee.

BP ID	BR ID	Business Rule
BP-004	BR-025	An individual customer whose total delinquent payment amount is greater than $250 must not schedule new services.
BP-004	BR-026	An organizational customer whose total delinquent payment amount is greater than $750 must not schedule new services.
BP-005	BR-027	The requested service date must be equal to or greater than the service availability date.
BP-005	BR-028	A requested service location (postal code) must be within an area serviced by SK on the requested service date.
BP-009	BR-030	A property type discount for a new scheduled job is based on the customer's total paid services in the past 12 calendar months. See Decision Table 08 for discount percentages.
BP-010	BR-032	A job canceled less than one business day prior to the Job's scheduled date must be charged a cancellation fee.

Business Process Diagram

A business process diagram shows the flows between related actions needed to achieve a valued result.

Usefulness

This model is useful for analyzing the flow of the actions in any view (Big-View, Pre-View, Now-View). The use of rows, also called swim lanes, indicates who or what performs the actions.

Example

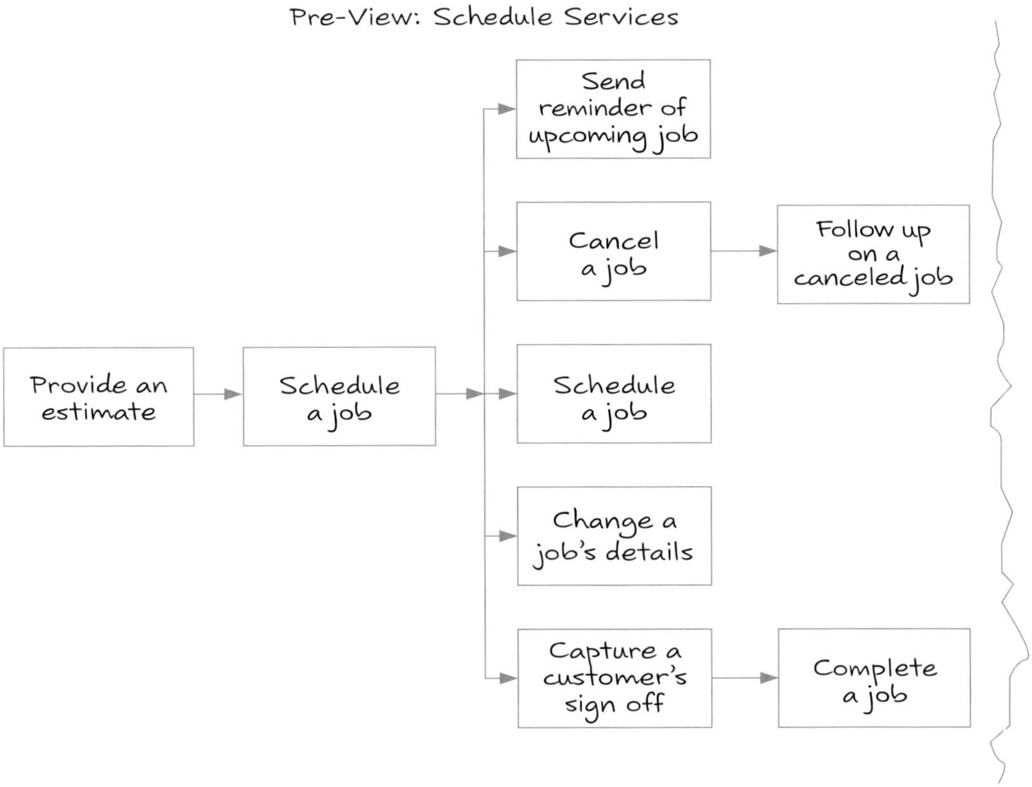

Capability Map

A capability map identifies your organization's business capabilities: a combination of business functions, people (organization, skills, and knowledge), technologies, and assets (money and facilities) that generates value for customers.

Usefulness

This model is useful when you're developing strategies for investing in process improvement and technology. It can help you understand how to align your information technology services with your business capabilities, and it can help you to decide which capabilities you might outsource. It's also useful for developing a rationale for project and program investments.

Capabilities can be mapped in a variety of ways: grouped by type (strategic, value-added, enabling), decomposed into subsets, or supplemented with relevant attributes (customer, owner, location, service level agreements, performance levels, and so on). Capability gaps can be illustrated with a *capability heat map* highlighting value, performance gaps, and risks.

Example

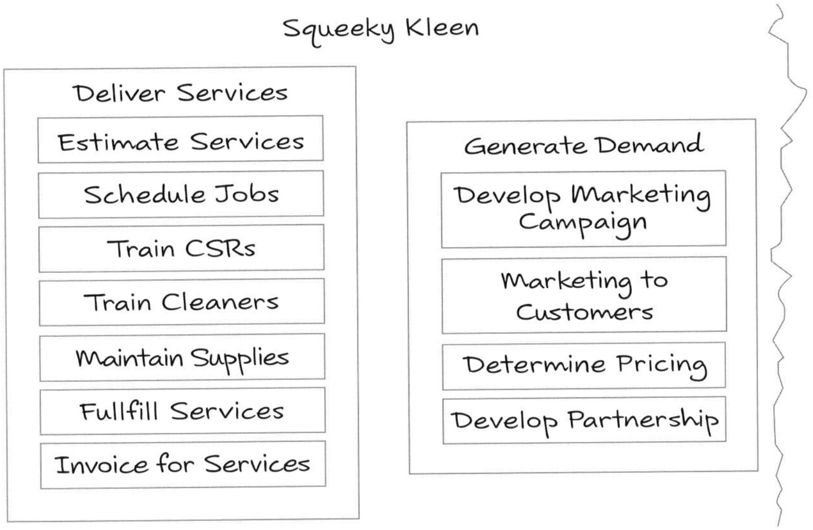

Context Diagram

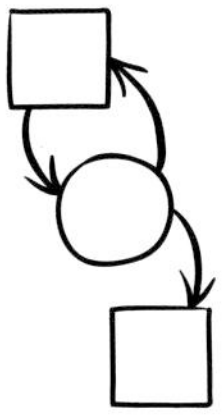

A context diagram logically illustrates interfaces by showing a product or portion of a product in its environment along with the external entities (people, systems, devices) that send data to the product, and receive data from it.

Usefulness

A context diagram clarifies boundaries for what is outside the product (external entities) and describes the communications (interfaces) between the product and those external entities. Early identification of the interfaces lets you synchronize activities with the interfacing parties, including planning, design, development, testing, and deployment. This collaboration is especially important for system-to-system interfaces.

A context diagram may be drawn to visualize interfaces at any planning view.

Example

Pre-View

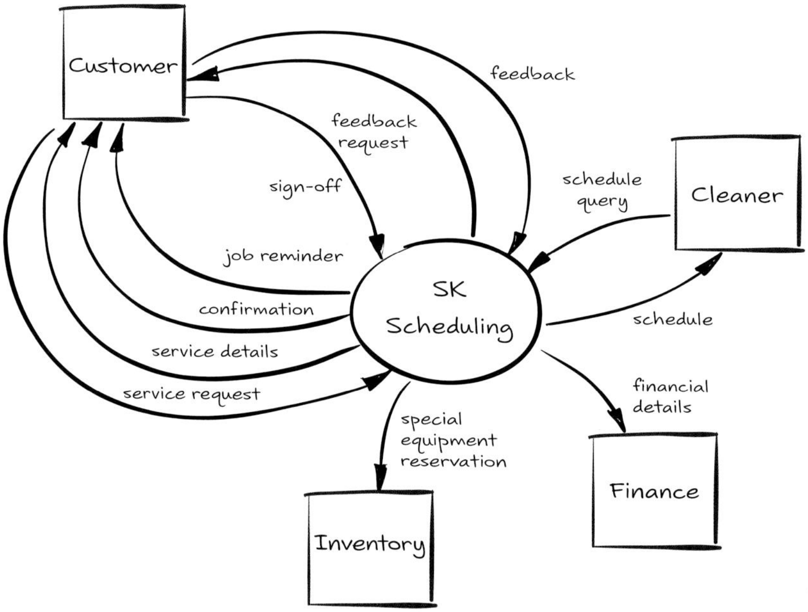

Contextual Inquiry

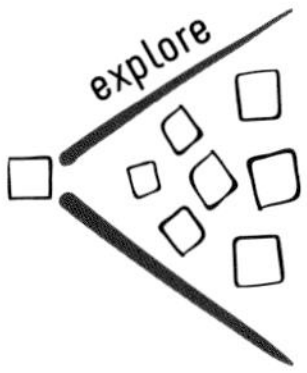

Contextual inquiry studies users in their environment, eliciting details about what they do in order to understand their needs.

Usefulness

By observing the product's users in their environment, you learn the context of use, you identify the user's goals, and you may discover tacit needs—those not explicitly expressed or openly declared.

Contextual inquiry provides detailed, qualitative data useful for ongoing discovery and delivery cycles (Beyer and Holtzblatt, 1997). It is collaborative; you reconstruct user tasks using visual models and converse with users to interpret the models. It is flexible and can be done anywhere the user is located.

Example

Notes from observing CSRs working in the SK office.
Open office space. CSRs assigned to short-walled cubicle; shared with another part-time CSR (they work different hours).

- Typical CSR desk with:
  - Large computer, display monitor, mouse, keyboard
  - Telephone (CSRs also have headsets)
  - Large calculator
  - Various sticky posts, pens, paperclips
- On cubicle wall:
  - Map with SK's service areas highlighted
  - Sketches of various types of windows with handwritten notes
  - Phone numbers – cleaners
  - List of cleaning prices
- Software:
  - Spreadsheet of prices
  - Simple database of customer and property details
  - Access to Internet limited. The most frequently used site provides maps and driving directions.

continued on next page

In shared area next to office manager's desk:

- Printer, fax machine, scanner
- Binder that contains descriptions of window and door types
- Supply closet
- Workstation for cleaners to use when in the office

Used before, during and after observation:

- Persona (Charlie, Customer Service Rep)
- Business process diagram
- Scenarios

Data Attribute, Data Dictionary

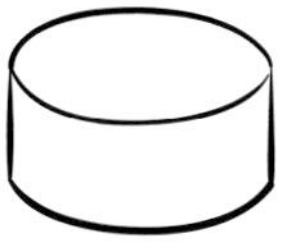

A data attribute is an aspect of data that is specific to a data entity needed to support business activities. Attributes may be shown on a data model or listed in a data dictionary (or both).

A data dictionary is a catalog of the data attributes that a product needs.

Usefulness

Identifying and defining the product's data attributes provide details used when you're writing business rules, creating prototypes, confirming expected results. A data dictionary provides a repository for detailed data used by the stakeholders.

Examples

Attributes shown in data model

Job
number scheduled date scheduled time status canceled date

Data Dictionary

Entity	Attribute	Definition	Data type	Length	Example / Valid values	Mandatory /Optional
Job	number	unique ID	numeric	9	555555555	m
Job	scheduled date	date for...	date	8	20121130	m
Job	scheduled time	when to expect cleaner...	charac-ter	20	8-12 a.m., 12-3 p.m., 3 p.m.-6 p.m.	m
Job	status	current standing	charac-ter	15	scheduled, unfinished, signed-off, completed, canceled, paid	m
Job	canceled date	date canceled	date	8	20121105	m when status= canceled

Data Domain, Data Entity

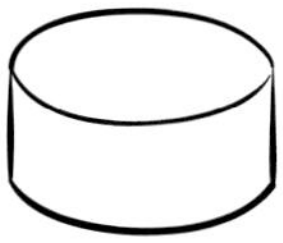

A data domain is any important topic that a product acts on and needs to remember.

A data entity represents a group of related pieces of information to be stored by the system. The entity can be about people, roles, places, things, organizations, occurrences in time, concepts, or documents.

Usefulness

Defining your data domains and data entities gives you a high-level understanding of the product's data needs.

Example

Data Domain	Data Entity
Agreement	Estimate Job
Party	Cleaner Customer Customer Service Representative (CSR) External Financial Party Wholesale Distributor
Financial	Coupon Deposit Payment Location Tax
Location	Property
Provider	Financial Institution Wholesale Distributor
Service	Service Area Service Type Property Type

Data Example

A data example provides concrete, specific data used to explore, evaluate, and confirm product needs.

Usefulness

Clearly defined data examples help you to explore data, clarify business rules, and specify expected results. You can use data examples as the basis for structuring and writing acceptance tests.

Example 1

Service Area postal code	Service Area start availability date	Service Area end availability date
12345	2012-01-01	n/a
13333	2011-08-01	2012-06-01
14444	2012-10-01	n/a

Example 2

Business rule: A property's postal code must match a service area's postal code serviced by SK on the requested date.

Scenario	Input Data: property postal code	Input Data: requested date	Expected Result
Property matches service area for requested date	12345	2012-10-15	Message: The property is in an area currently serviced by SK.
Property does not match service area for requested date	22222	2012-12-19	Message: The property is not in an area currently serviced by SK.
Property no longer matches SK's service area	13333	2012-11-23	Message: The property is in an area no longer serviced by SK.
Property will match an SK service area in near future	14444	2012-10-05	Message: SK will begin to offer services in this area starting October 1, 2012.

Data Model, Conceptual Data Model, Logical Data Model

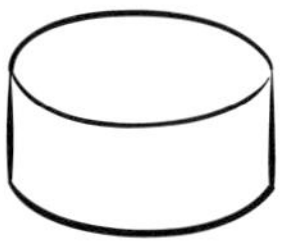

A data model shows the logical structures of data—domains (or entities) and relationships—independently of the data design. It is also known as a *fact model*.

A conceptual data model is a high-level visual model of six to ten important data domains or entities and their relationships (it may or may not include the relationships' optionality and cardinality).

A logical data model is a comprehensive rendering of the detailed data requirements needed to support behavior, control, and interface requirements. It typically includes rules that define the relationships' optionality and cardinality.

A data relationship is a business rule that links two data domains or entities—for example, Job is paid by Customer Payment. You can further qualify the relationship by using multiplicity symbols to indicate the relationship's optionality and cardinality rules.

An inheritance hierarchy shows the types of an entity. A supertype entity encapsulates data and relationships that are common to all types in that class. A subtype entity details its unique attributes and relationships. A subtype inherits its supertype's attributes and relationships. The relationship between the subtype and the supertype is named "is a"—for example, "an organization is a customer."

Usefulness

A data model provides a structure you can use to discover and organize data. It gives team members a common vocabulary that permeates other Dimensions (Actions, Controls, Interfaces, and User).

Examples

Conceptual Data Model

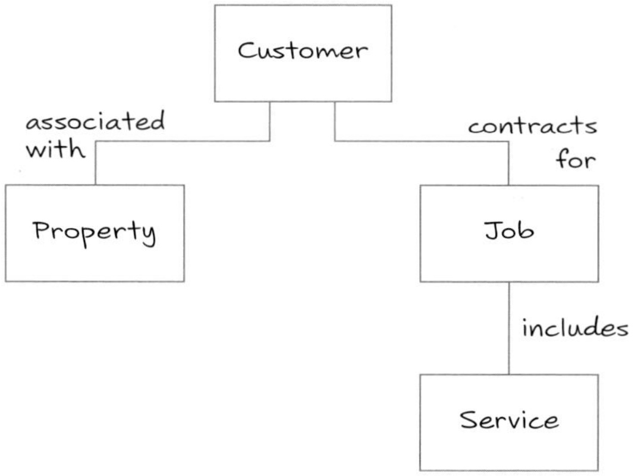

Logical Data Model

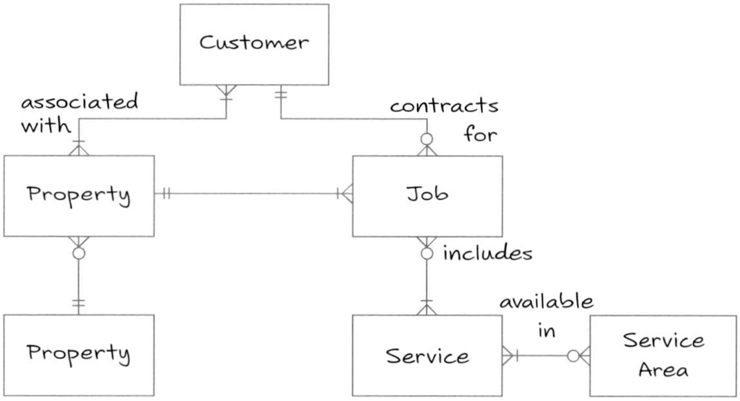

Data Model: Inheritance Hierarchy

Decision Table, Decision Tree

A decision table specifies a set of conditions to reach a business conclusion. Data representing the premise, antecedent, or condition is paired with the conclusion or consequence data.

A decision tree illustrates a set of conditions to reach a business conclusion.

Usefulness

A decision table or tree helps you organize and confirm (test) a cohesive set of business rules. You use a decision table when the rules share a significant number of parallels—same subject, purpose, or pattern—and a finite number of relevant values.

Examples

BR-030: The property type discount for new scheduled job is based on the customer's total paid services in the past 12 calendar months.

Decision Table 08: Property Type Discount Percentages

Property type	Total paid services	Discount %
Residential	0–$249	0%
Residential	$250–$499	3%
Residential	$500–$999	5%
Residential	>$1000	7%
Commercial	0–$999	0%
Commercial	$1000–$2999	5%
Commercial	$3000–$4999	7%
Commercial	>$5000	10%

Decision Tree 12: Property Type Discount Percentages

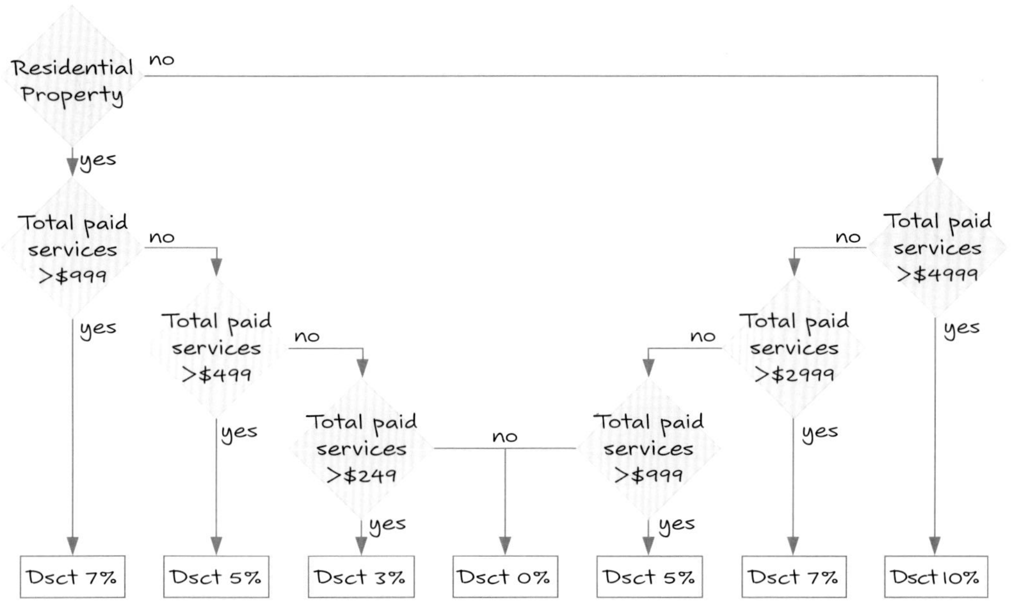

Dependency Graph

A dependency graph visualizes relationships between elements in which one element (the client) requires or depends on another element (the supplier).

The graph shows the actions with directed arrows from the client action to the supplier action.

The dependency graph does not represent usage flow of actions. For this, you use a story map or business process diagram.

Usefulness

Analyzing how a *precondition* of one action is satisfied by a *postcondition* of another action in any view (Big-View, Pre-View, Now-View) is essential when you allocate high-value product options to plans, releases, and software components.

Example

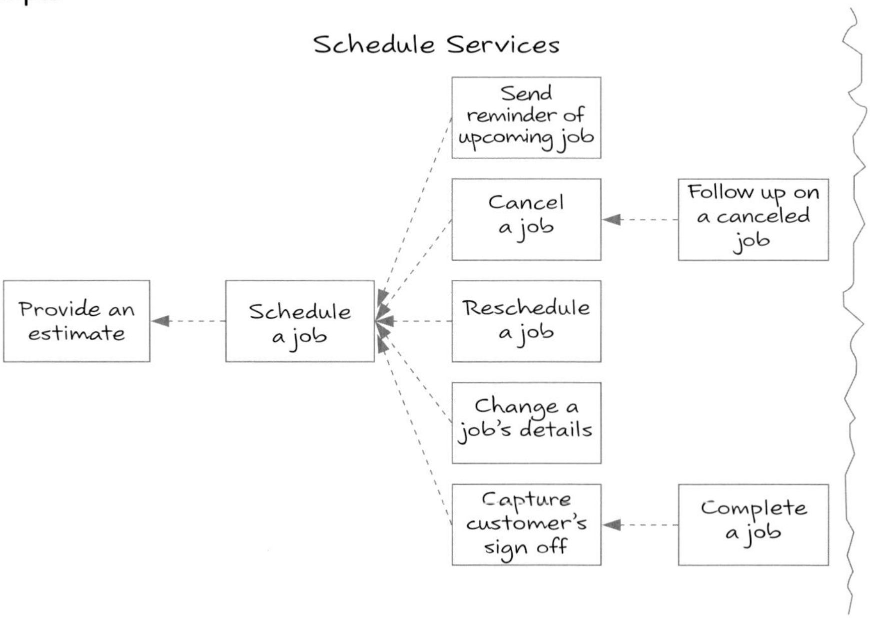

Event and Response

An event is a trigger that causes the business to respond. A response is a predefined action.

A user initiates a business event. A temporal event is triggered at a specified time, as defined or required by a product partner.

Usefulness

Identifying and analyzing relevant events is an efficient way to initially define the system's scope. You can use event-responses as a way to discover features, MMFs, use cases, or stories. You can prioritize events to help allocate event-responses to planning horizons.

Example

Event	Response
Customer wants to learn about SK services and locations.	Search for services and locations.
Customer contacts SK to arrange for services.	Schedule a job.
Cleaner reports the job is completed.	Charge the customer for services.
Time to order supplies.	Send order to supplier.
Time to follow up with customer.	Request feedback on services.

Facilitated Workshop

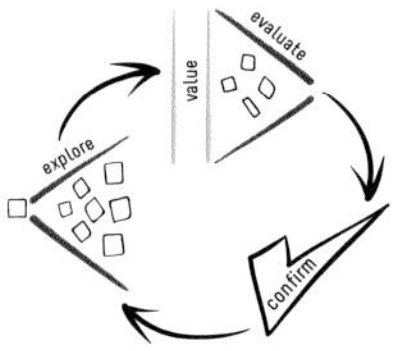

A facilitated workshop is a structured meeting in which product partners collaborate to plan and analyze product needs with the guidance of a skilled, neutral facilitator.

Usefulness

Facilitated workshops help you to obtain diverse viewpoints in a safe, structured setting and conduct complex, efficient conversations that result in decisions for action.

By having a neutral facilitator to plan, design, and facilitate workshops, you free the product partners to focus on the content of their conversations, stay actively engaged, transparently raise diverse opinions, and communicate effectively (Gottesdiener, 2002). A neutral facilitator is especially critical with larger groups where there are many viewpoints. The facilitator uses a variety of techniques that promote mutual understanding, shared learning, commitment, and trust.

Example

Pre-View (Release Planning) Workshop

Purpose	Discover product options and define a plan for the next release
Participants (Product Partners)	Customer: Ray and Pat (voice of the CSR user) Business: Pat (product champion) Technology: Deb, Lee, Ted Facilitator: Ben
Principles	• Use the Options board to build shared understanding. • Use decision rules and decision-making process. • Use value criteria, benefits, and risks to make value decisions. • Use acceptance criteria to confirm product options and define expected outcomes for each delivery cycle. • Hold one conversation at a time.

continued on next page

Products	Input • Product vision, market research information • Retrospective feedback from prior delivery cycles • Contextual inquiry research findings • CSR persona • Glossary of SK domain terms • Draft release theme Output • High-level release plan; candidate solutions (stories), acceptance criteria • Release theme, risks, and list of dependencies • Options board and analysis models, e.g. context diagram, business process diagram, user role map, data model, etc. • Actions and next steps • Workshop retrospective feedback
Process (Agenda)	1. Set the context: Review the product vision, new market research information, contextual inquiry research, and prior delivery cycle retrospective feedback. Review the state of the product architecture. Revise, if needed, value criteria. Share the next release's theme and acceptance criteria. 2. Conduct structured conversation: Explore and evaluate, using the Options board. Select high-value options and identify next release's stories, write story acceptance criteria. Use examples and analysis models. 3. Plan (allocate high-value options): Identify the release theme, risks, and dependencies. Estimate stories, adjust options as needed, write release acceptance criteria. Review the plan using high-level scenarios and adjust the plan as needed. 4. Workshop wrap and retrospective: Identify actions and next steps, and conduct workshop retrospective.

Feature, Minimum Marketable Feature (MMF), Minimum Viable Product (MVP)

A feature is a cohesive bundle of externally visible functionality that aligns with business goals and objectives. Each feature is a logically related grouping of functional and nonfunctional product needs described in broad strokes (Gottesdiener, 2005).

A minimum marketable feature (MMF) is the smallest set of functionality that is valued by customers and returns value when independently released (Denne and Cleland-Huang, 2003). "Minimum" is the smallest possible subset of options, "marketable" has value to a customer who buys or uses it, and "feature" provides externally visible functionality. A candidate solution may be one or more MMFs (or, if fine-grained, a candidate solution might be a story).

Depending on view and granularity, a set of MMFs (or a feature or candidate solution) may be considered a *minimum viable product* (MVP).

Usefulness

A feature provides a concise and efficient way to represent a set of product options.

An MMF is a means of clustering actions based on market value.

Examples

Features
- Self-service scheduling
- Instant pay

MMFs
- Online customer self-service cleaning estimate
- Online customer self-service cleaning schedule
- Instant pay discount when scheduling
- Instant pay at job completion using mobile device

Given-When-Then

Given-When-Then is a way to express a scenario with data, including pre- and postconditions.

Usefulness

You use Given-When-Then to explore and confirm product options. It enables business, customer, and technology partners to communicate using business domain language. It also serves as a test case for acceptance testing.

At the Pre-View level, you can use Given-When-Then to outline the release's expected outcomes.

At the Now-View level, each atomic Given-When-Then is focused on a scenario for one story, one specific user, and one business rule.

Example

Story	As a Customer, I need to verify my service location is within SK service area, so...
Scenario	Requested service location is within service area for requested date.
Business rule	A requested service location (postal code) must be within an area supported by SK on the requested service date.
Given	
precondition(s), state	Service Locations exist
fixed data	Service Location postal code: 12345 Service Location start availability date: 2009-01-01
When	
action	Verify requested service location
input data	Service requested date: 2012-11-30 Property location postal code: 12345
Then	
observable outcome: message, output data	Message: The property is in an area currently serviced by SK
postcondition(s)	n/a

Glossary

A glossary is a collection of the business terms and concepts relevant to the product, along with their definitions.

Usefulness

A glossary enables stakeholders to communicate using a shared language. It provides a single source for terms to be used throughout product discovery and delivery.

Example

Term	Definition	Aliases	Examples
Commercial Property	Real estate intended to generate a profit.		Office building
Customer	A party (individual or organization) that contracts for services with SK.	Client	Roger Smith
Estimate	A statement from SK that provides the likely cost of a job.	Quote	
Job	An agreement between SK and the customer wherein SK provides services at a specific property on a specific day, and the customer provides payment upon completion of services.	Work order, service request	Clean the outside of 25 pane windows, 3 mirrors, and 1 skylight on morning of March 13
Property Location	The physical location where services are provided.	Job location	123 Main Street, Anytown, Country
Quote	See estimate	Estimate	
Wholesale Distributor	A business organization that sells manufacturers' products to commercial users.		

Interaction Matrix

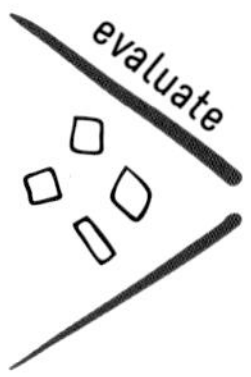

An interaction matrix is a means to explore, evaluate, and confirm the expected effects of actions on data.

Rows: Action dimension's features, or MMFs, or stories
Columns: Data dimension's data domains or data entities
Cell: Effect of the action on relevant data: create, read, update, delete

Usefulness

Analyzing the impact of an action on data clarifies the scope of the work you're considering and identifies any dependencies between the action and data.

- For an action: What data does it utilize? Are there missing data? Does the action need to read data that is created in another application or product?
- For data: What actions affect the data? Are there missing actions needed to support the data?

Understanding the impact of these interactions helps you to allocate product options within a release and across releases. The natural order of planning is to allocate actions that create data before you allocate actions that read, update, or delete that data. When the plan doesn't support that progression, you may need to (temporarily) fabricate the needed data.

Example

Action / Data	Customer	Job	Property	Service
Customer schedules a job	Create (if new) Read (if existing) Update (if existing)	Create	Create (if new) Read (if existing) Update (if existing)	Read
Customer cancels a job		Update		
Search for services				Read
Send reminder about an upcoming job	Read	Read		

Options Board

An Options board is a visual space, usually mounted on a wall, used by a team to explore and evaluate product options

Usefulness

An Options board provides a foundation for creating plans at various horizons. It is useful when you're preparing for planning sessions, during planning sessions, and throughout iterations and releases as you converse about candidate solutions. By making the options visible to everyone, an Options board promotes collaboration, innovation, shared understanding, and trust (Gottesdiener, 2002).

The format can vary. Typically, the 7 Product Dimensions are arrayed horizontally across a wall, with product options shown beneath each respective dimension. You can list options as text, visual analysis models, or both (see this section for a variety of ways to represent product dimensions). Because people often communicate powerfully and quickly by using a combination of words and pictures, both are typically used.

An Options board is a good way to document decisions about each option's value. For example, you might draw a star next to high-value options, or circle or highlight them. When participants are distributed, you might want to use collaboration technologies such as software and video tools. An Options board might also include a list of the product partners, along with their value considerations.

Example

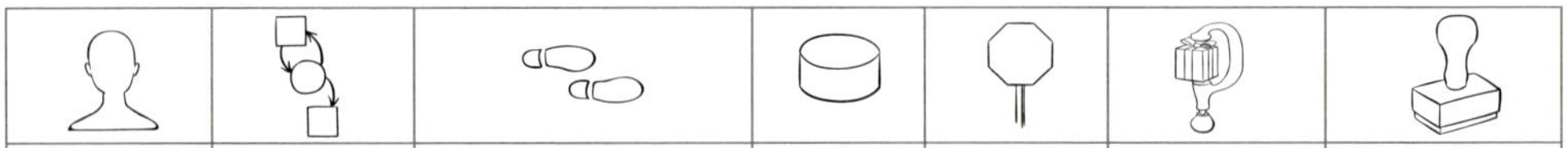

User	Interface	Action	Data	Control	Environment	Quality Attribute
Estimator Role* CSR* CSR state* Junior*	Customer to CSR* request details verbal *	Provide estimate* verify requested location* select window type* display window type description display window type image	Coupon Discount Estimate* window type	Estimate is an approximate price*	SK Office* Database* BigBox Relational ElephantOpen SourceDataStorage*	Usability* Amount of time to provide estimate with no help...

Due to space limitations we show only a part of the Options board here.

See www.DiscoverToDeliver.com for samples.

Persona

A persona is a written description of a typical user's background, including relevant details such as needs and goals.

Usefulness

Creating personas is a way to learn about the users' behaviors, context, background, and goals, in any view (Big-View, Pre-View, Now-View). Personas are useful for identifying interactions with the product and evaluating options, especially decisions about user interface design.

Example

Persona Name: Charlie, a junior Customer Service Rep (CSR)

Description 	In constant communication with customers and contractors. Must satisfy customers' needs in timely, courteous way. Includes all activities surrounding customer jobs: scheduling, canceling, rescheduling, etc. Acts as liaison with Accounting. "A good day is when I can respond to 90% of new customer requests within 3 minutes." Part-time employee of SK, paid by the hour, receives bonuses when exceeds service level agreements. Knowledgeable about business, maintains good relationship with cleaners. Amiable, problem solver, proficient with standard office software products.
Needs	Easy access to essential, up-to-date customer and property data. Rapid way to communicate with cleaners. Relief from mundane tasks, e.g., reminding customer of upcoming job.
Goals	Provide efficient and personal service. Exceed SK's service level agreements to earn bonus.

Planguage

Planguage is a keyword-driven language designed to specify product needs quantitatively in natural language.

Usefulness

Planguage is an extensible, flexible framework (Gilb, 2005). It can be used to consistently and precisely define functional and nonfunctional product dimensions, acceptance criteria, and business value.

Example

Quality Attribute: SK scheduling functionality must be available during regular workdays with minimal downtime.

Gist	Availability.SchedulingCSRaccess
Scale	Percentage of time the system is available for scheduling jobs
Meter	Calculate percent of time available during working hours, excluding company-specified holidays. Working hours are defined as: Monday through Friday from 8:00 a.m. to 5:00 p.m. Eastern time, Saturday 8:00 a.m. to 2 p.m. Eastern time
Minimum	95%
Plan	98%

Plan

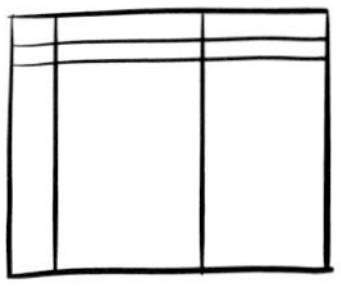

A plan is the partners' best estimates of what might be delivered during a given planning horizon to achieve value.

Usefulness

Plans align people and resources to business goals and objectives for a given planning horizon. Plans support a theme or crucial product feature or milestone by showing features, MMFs, or stories in order of priority (value), adjusted for dependencies and risks. By planning continually, you can make timely adjustments based on anticipated versus actual value, customer feedback, and planned versus delivered product options.

Big-View Product roadmap; Portfolio roadmap	Product roadmaps help business and technology stakeholders to agree on strategic direction. Big-View planning encourages business and technology partners to collaborate to identify a technology roadmap. Internal roadmaps encourage partners to understand customers and their needs, communicate the product vision and the needed actions, align people and resources to the vision, promote collaboration, and establish value considerations for ongoing decision making. External roadmaps help you gain or retain customers by lending credibility, communicating strategy, and establishing market leadership.
Pre-View Release plan; Product queue	Release plans align people and resources with a theme or crucial product feature and coordinate features and dependencies across multiple teams.
Now-View Iteration, sprint plan (timebox delivery); Product queue (flow delivery)	Iteration plans help you to converse about product options for the immediate delivery cycle. An iteration or release plan helps you visualize current work-in-progress and monitor and manage the stages of the work, enabling you to reduce risk and deliver product options faster. Using task or workflow visualization for the Now-View alerts you to issues, signals risks and problems in real time, increases daily team learning, informs management when team impediments need immediate attention, improves a team's ability to continually improve its practices, and reduces cycle time.

Examples

Example 1: Big-View Product Roadmap

Theme	Easy Estimator	Trust Me	Show Me the Money
Release	1	2	3
Candidate Solutions	Off-site cleaning estimates Self-service hypothesis (24x7)	Optimize scheduling Self-service cleaning estimates On-site cleaning estimates	Self-service cleaning scheduling Repair service hypothesis Instant pay Accounting package

Example 2: Big-View Product Roadmap

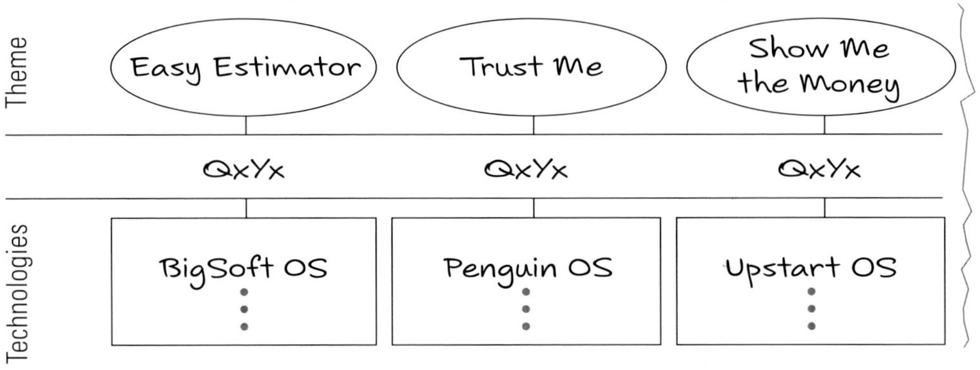

Plan Elements

Typically a plan communicates product options using the Action Dimension. A common format is to place actions (features, MMFs, or stories) in rows, allocated to a column that indicates the delivery timeframe. For Big-View and Pre-View plans, the columns represent the date or timeframe for delivery. For Now-View plans, the columns are the state of the work-in-progress.

Agile/Lean project teams plan continually, revising plans based on customer feedback, actual versus estimated cycle time (or velocity), changing team capacity, and ever-unfolding business conditions and risks. Multiple shorter-term plans are nested within longer-term plans and updated with each delivery cycle. Multiple plans are used to show how project deliveries extend across planning views, helping you visualize how product needs will be progressively realized and delivered.

Plan elements and organizing schemes vary based on your preferences, planning horizon, known dependencies, and delivery method. Plans at any view can include a theme or goal, the key persona benefiting from the feature or stories, and a timeline.

Plan Views

Plans use a timeline or cadence. A regular cadence might be scheduled (once a week, every two weeks, once a quarter) or align to the partners' planning cycle (quarterly, annually). A varied cadence may be tied to projected market events or cycles (partner or market conferences or customer sign-ups).

Shorter-term plans can include attributes such as estimated size, estimated delivery date or completion time, needed tasks, risks, person assigned, state of the item (e.g., in progress, in a queue awaiting further work, completed), problem indicators (such as the item being "blocked" or on hold due to a delay or problem), dependencies, and so on.

Product Vision

A product vision articulates the long-term concept of a product.

Usefulness

The product vision gives you a concise, coherent, and unifying basis for choosing among competing product options, clarifying product scope, and communicating with internal and external partners. The vision can outline the product's key benefits or purpose, its differentiators and advantages, and its contribution to your strategy.

Generating a crisp, compelling product vision requires disciplined thinking. The partners incorporate diverse perspectives on value considerations, features, customers, and strategy to reach agreement on the core guiding vision for ongoing product decisions.

The format of the product vision can be visual (an image or diagram illustrating how the product affects its customers), tangible (a box with vision elements placed on it), textual (using a standard template or newspaper headline format), or a combination.

Examples

Vision Statement for Squeeky Kleen

Text, Short Form

To be a trusted partner for reliable, safe, and competitively priced cleaning.

Text, Longer Form

For Squeeky Kleen customers
Who need glass cleaning services for residential or commercial properties
Squeeky Kleen's "Kleer View" is a software product
That supports answering inquiries, estimating and scheduling cleaning jobs, assigning staff to perform the services, replenishing supplies, supporting compliance activities, and managing financial transactions.
Unlike the existing combination of software tools and manual processes
Our "Kleer View" product will support full life-cycle business services.
(Based on Moore, 2006)

Prototype

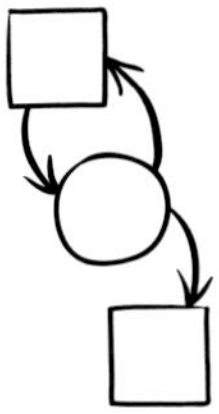

A prototype is a representation of a product. A prototype of a user interface might be represented by using wireframes or detailed mock-ups. A low-fidelity prototype might be drawn on paper or laid out on a whiteboard with sticky notes, or drawn in a software tool. A higher-fidelity prototype might be a fully functioning piece of software.

Usefulness

Prototypes enable users to envision and experience the product's outwardly observable possibilities and limitations. Prototypes can give you early and rapid feedback to help you discover product options when user experience is highly valued. Prototypes help you explore other product dimensions (User, Action, Data, Control, Environment, Quality Attribute) and actively engage customers.

Example

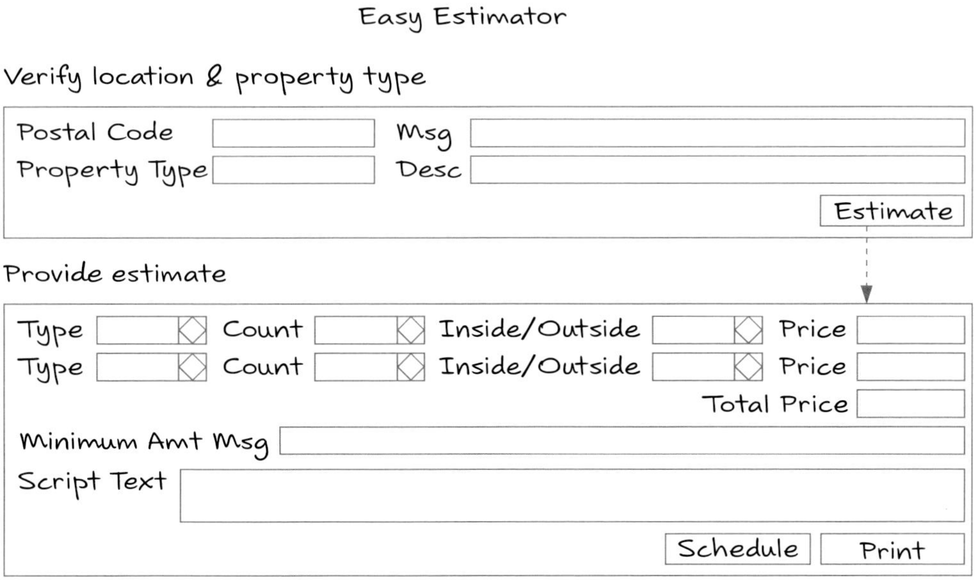

Quality Attribute Scenario

A quality attribute scenario characterizes quality attributes as high-level scenarios using a templated specification.

Usefulness

Quality attribute scenarios provide an extensible framework to consistently define quality attributes (Barbacci et al. 2003, and Bass et al. 2001). It provides an alternative way, using sentences, to specify the quality attributes.

Example

Junior CSR completes scheduling a residential window job for an existing customer within five minutes.

Source	Junior service scheduler
Stimulus	Existing customer requests window cleaning for their residential property
Artifact	Job scheduling interface
Environment	Five CSRs online at same time using the application
Response	Scheduling confirmation emailed to the customer
Response measure	No more than three minutes for 80% of requests, no more than eight minutes for the remaining 20%

Relationship Map

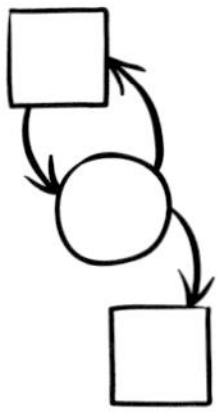

A relationship map shows the relationships that exist among the organization's functions and with external entities (customers and providers).

Usefulness

A relationship map helps you understand organizational interfaces by illustrating the information flows among the entire cross-functional organization, as well as to and from external entities. It provides a meta-level view of the boundaries, typically at the Big-View.

Example

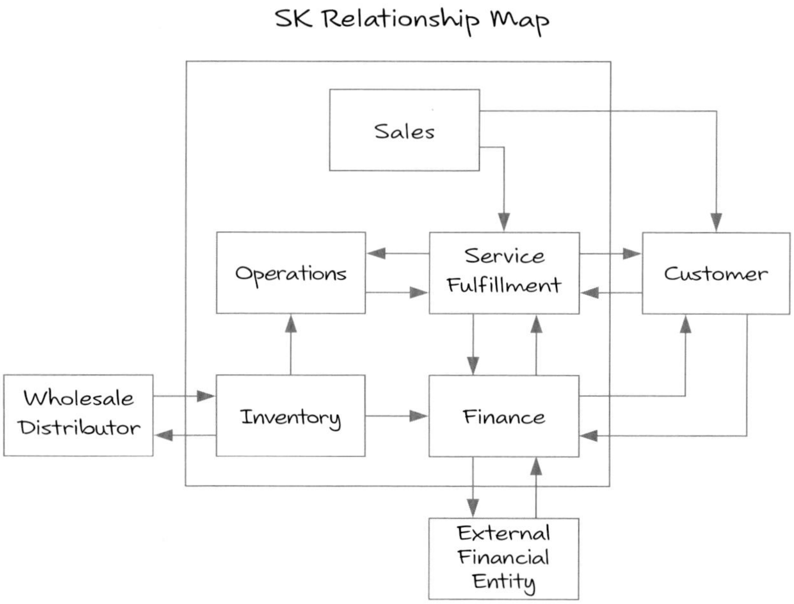

Scenario

A scenario is a text description of an instance of use.

Usefulness

Scenarios help you validate product needs in any view (Big-View, Pre-View, Now-View) and generate acceptance criteria and acceptance tests in the Now-View.

Examples

Big-View

Roger Smith has just purchased a new property and needs help getting it cleaned. He checks with Squeeky Kleen to learn about its services and get an estimate. A few days later Roger calls back to schedule the cleaning work. After the job is completed, Squeeky Kleen bills Roger for the services. When his payment is received, a Squeeky Kleen representative follows up with Roger to make sure he is satisfied and to offer him a discount coupon for future services.

Pre-View

Roger Smith, an individual customer, schedules window cleaning at his residential property. SK verifies his credit, schedules a cleaner, creates a cleaning "pick list," and reserves any special equipment. Roger receives a confirmation with all the details, including the cancellation policy.

Now-View

Roger Smith wants to schedule window cleaning for next Saturday morning, but no cleaner is available for that day.

Scenario Z Pattern

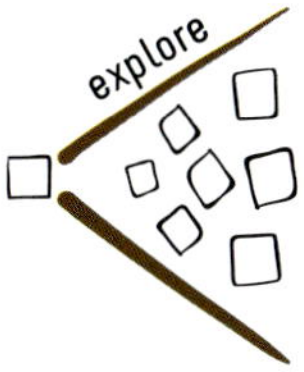

The Scenario Z pattern uses scenarios as a path to explore options across planning views.

Usefulness

In the Scenario Z pattern, you navigate from one planning view to another by using concrete scenarios. A high-value scenario in one planning view serves as a starting point to explore an option at the subsequent planning view. The pattern is useful for exploring any product dimension, although it is more commonly used for the Action Dimension.

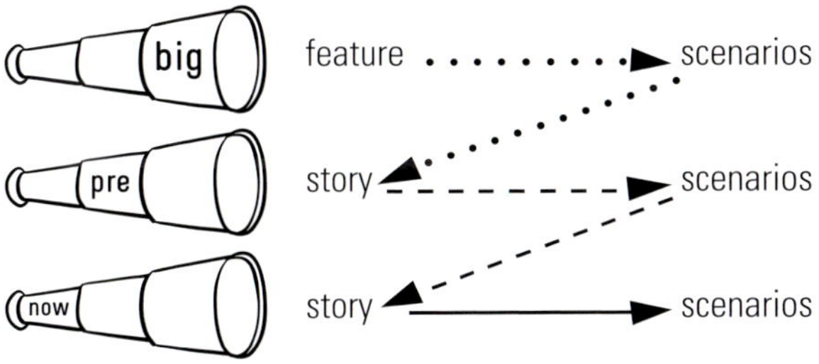

Example

View	Action	Scenario
Big-View	Estimate price of services	commercial property cleaning services commercial property repair services residential property cleaning services residential property repair services
Pre-View	Estimate price of residential property cleaning services	nonstandard residential window cleaning standard residential solar panel cleaning standard residential gutter cleaning standard residential window cleaning
Now-View	Estimate price of window cleaning services for standard residential property	includes all taxes does not include any taxes total price > 5K minimum price total price < 5K minimum price single window type estimated multiple window types estimated

State Diagram

A state is a defined condition of a data entity or user role.

A state diagram shows the allowable transitions from one data state to another.

Usefulness

A state diagram is a simple, powerful way to analyze a data entity's scope. The state diagram provides a visual means to explore the life cycle of a data entity and the actions that transition it from state to state.

Examples

States of the Job

Scheduled	Paid
Canceled	Signed-off
Completed	Unfinished

State Diagram of the Job

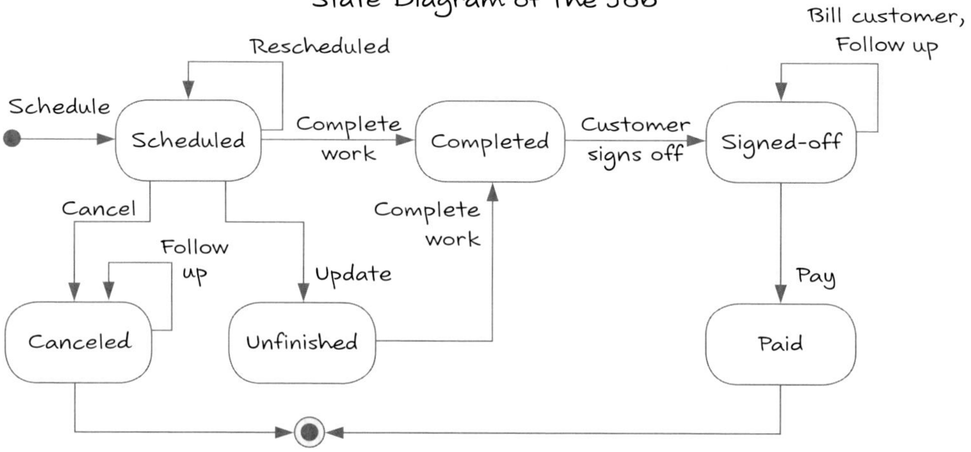

Story

A story is a product need expressed as a user's goal. A story can be catalogued in a queue or product backlog.

When used at the Now-View, a story is an assembly of high-value options across the 7 Product Dimensions and is small enough for the delivery team to develop within the Now-View's time horizon. Typically, a Now-View story is associated with multiple detailed scenarios and acceptance criteria.

Usefulness

A story serves as a communication channel between the person with the need (the user) and the development team that will realize the story. Stories help to define business value. They serve as a way to partition actions and explore dependencies.

Examples

Pre-View Story

Sch 07 Schedule a job
As an existing customer I need to schedule window cleaning services
so I can make arrangements to be home when the cleaner arrives.

Estimate: medium Date story identified: 06-20

Now-View Story

Sch 14 Reschedule a job
As a customer I need to change the date and time my windows will be cleaned
so it is more convenient for me.

Estimate: small Date story identified: 06-25

Story Map

A story map organizes stories in logical order using two dimensions: usage sequence (left to right) and business importance (stories listed in vertical order of value, with most valuable at the top).

Usefulness

A story map is a way to visualize stories in a cohesive structure that aids in evaluating, prioritizing, and allocating stories to a plan.

Example

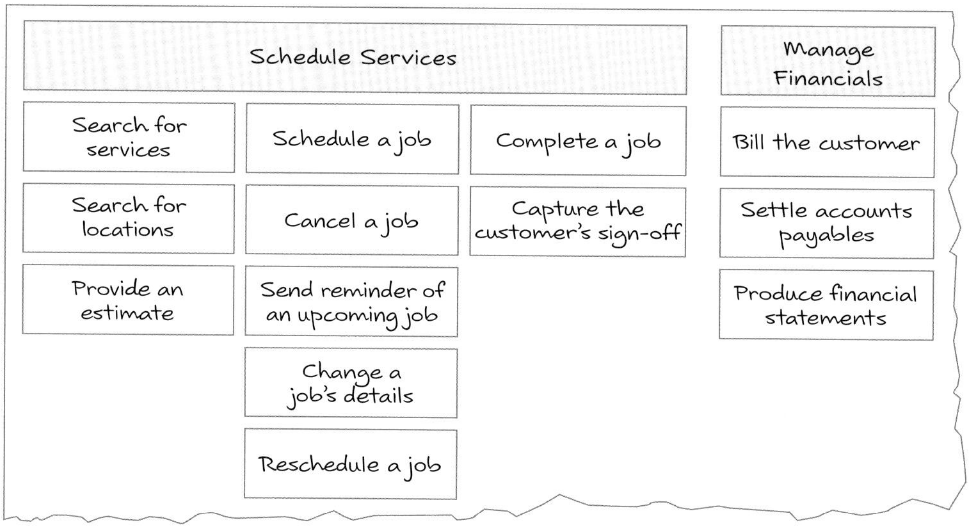

Use Case

A use case describes how a user's goal is achieved through interacting with a product.

Usefulness

A use case may be used to assemble a set of high-value stories. This assembly is helpful for testing the flow through the user's interactions. You can use the pre- and postconditions documented with use cases to analyze state dependencies.

Example

Name	Schedule a Job for an Existing Customer
Actor	Customer
Triggering event	Customer contacts SK to arrange for services
Precondition	Customer exists
Postcondition	Job is scheduled
Actor action	System response
Check location	Verify that requested location is within SK's service area.
Check a service	Verify that requested service is provided by SK.
Request price	Calculate price for requested service.
	Confirm price with customer.
Check schedule availability	Find available cleaner to perform service.
Provide payment details	Verify payment method.
	Verify credit card details.
	Request job detail confirmation.
Confirm job details	Store job details.
	Send job confirmation to customer.
	Provide cancellation policy to customer.
	Provide liability policy to customer.
Confirm policies	Reserve any needed special equipment.

User, User Role, User Role Map

A user is a person, another product, or a system that interacts with a product to obtain value, participate in delivering value, or both. A user may be a person, another system, or a hardware device. High-value users are sometimes represented as personas.

Users may play many roles as they engage with the product. A user role represents a specific way that a user interacts with the product. Each user role has a specific goal.

A user role map visually represents the various types of user roles and the relationships among them.

Usefulness

Focusing on what a user needs to do (the user's roles) provides a stepping-stone to exploring actions.

A user role map is an efficient way to communicate a user's specialized subtypes. It is typically used in Pre-View and Now-View analysis.

Examples

Users at SK

Customer	Office Manager
CSR	Sales Staffer
Cleaner	Financial Staff

User Role Map

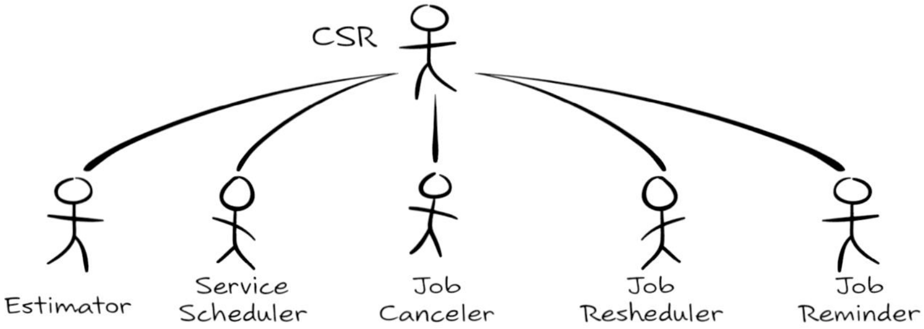

Value Stream Map

A value stream map shows the end-to-end sequence and movement of information, materials, and actions in the value stream.

Usefulness

Value stream mapping is a Lean manufacturing technique aimed at improving productivity. It can also help you improve discovery and delivery of products and services created as part of knowledge work.

This model helps you to understand how you collectively deliver value to customers, regardless of your organizational structure. By visualizing the current process, you can search for wasteful and unnecessary activities and then model the future state. A value stream map is useful for focusing on customer value and finding common activities, information, and materials you need in order to achieve valued customer results. This model helps you simplify complex activities and remove waste that adds no customer value.

When you're working on streamlining product development, you can modify the map to include simple graphics to represent materials and information.

Example

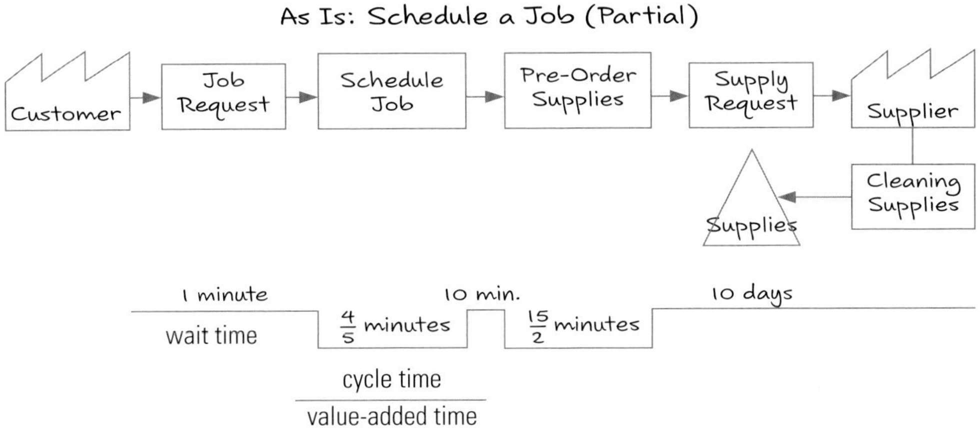

Value Tools

Value tools are qualitative or quantitative techniques useful for making value decisions about product options.

value

Value tools help to ensure that the product's options align with your strategy and are feasible, desirable, and financially viable. These tools help you assess product options against partners' considerations, such as organizational strategy, financial benefit and cost, market or product development risk, customer preference or demand, market differentiation, asset reuse, and more.

Usefulness

A variety of methods and tools can enrich your conversation about value, help you obtain multiple perspectives, and aid in making justifiable value decisions.
Some examples:

- Anderson Ranking
- Boston Box
- Economic Value Added
- Empathy Map
- Kano Model
- Net Promoter Score
- Prioritization Matrix
- Purpose Alignment Model
- Quality Function Deployment
- Return on Investment

Example

The Purpose Alignment Model is a matrix for categorizing business needs according to their alignment with the organization's mission and market differentiation (Pixton et al. 2009).

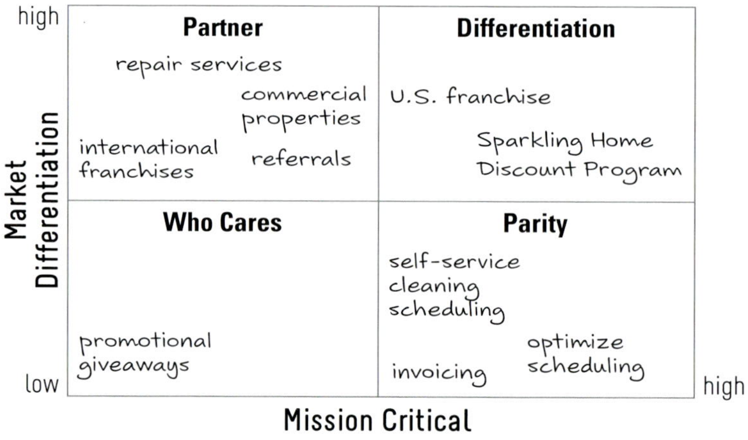

GLOSSARY

CASE STUDY

BIG CONCEPTS

7 DIMENSIONS

GLOSSARY

7 Dimensions: *see* 7 Product Dimensions.

7 Product Dimensions: aspects of a product (User, Interface, Action, Data, Control, Environment, and Quality Attribute Dimensions) that collectively provide a holistic, comprehensive understanding of the product.

A

acceptance criteria: concrete, unambiguous means used to verify and validate a candidate solution. Also called *conditions of satisfaction*, *doneness criteria*, and *doneness tests*.

acceptance criteria list: identifies what to test to validate a scenario, story, feature or candidate solution.

acceptance test: a means to confirm acceptance criteria.

Action Dimension: *see* Action Product Dimension.

Action Product Dimension: the product dimension that represents the capabilities a product provides to users.

actual results: results achieved in actual usage of a product that are used to validate whether the expected outcomes have been attained.

Agile: a software development framework for iterative development and incremental delivery of products, whereby a product and the process for building it undergo evolutionary change throughout the product life cycle.

Agile/Lean: an umbrella term describing the family of practices for building software and systems using iterative and incremental development and delivery, with a focus on maximizing customer value while minimizing waste. Also called Lean/Agile or Agile.

analysis model: a representation of product needs that may take the form of a diagram, list, or table, often supplemented with text.

availability: a quality attribute that defines when a product is accessible for use ("up time"). Includes factors such as backup, recovery, checkpoints, and restart.

B

Backlog: *see* product backlog.

backlog item: *see* product option.

benefit: an aspect of a product that favorably impacts the product's value to one or more product partners.

Big-View: the planning horizon that reflects the longest delivery cycle.

business model: a description of the rationale of the way an organization creates, delivers, and captures value. It can include discussion of revenue, costs, supplies, customer segments, partners, and distribution channels (Osterwalder and Pigneur, 2010).

business partner: *see* partner.

business policy: a principle or regulation that influences the behavior of an organization or product.

business process diagram: shows the flows between related actions needed to achieve a valued result for a specific customer.

business rule: a precise textual statement that defines, constrains, or enables the behavior of software, business processes, and data structures.

C

candidate solution: a cohesive assembly of high-value product options representing how the partners expect to achieve product goals. It may be represented or named as a feature, MMF, or use case.

capability: the ability to do something.

capability heat map: illustrates capability gaps in an organization by highlighting value, performance gaps, and risks. *See also* capability map.

capability map: identifies an organization's business capabilities: the combination of business functions, people, technologies, and assets that generates value for customers.

class of service: in Kanban, a way to categorize work. Used to determine how to treat the item to balance customer satisfaction with costs.

cohesive: the quality of being logically related or consistent.

commercial product: a product intended for sale to external customers.

conceptual data model: a high-level visual model of six to ten important data domains or entities and their relationships. *See also* data model.

conditions of satisfaction: *see* acceptance criteria.

context diagram: logically illustrates product scope by showing a product or a portion of a product in its environment, along with the external entities (people, systems, devices) that send data to the product and receive data from it.

contextual inquiry: studies users in their environment, eliciting details about what they do in order to understand their needs.

continuous flow: *see* flow.

Control Dimension: *see* Control Product Dimension.

Control Product Dimension: the product dimension that represents enforcement of constraints.

cross-cutting: in software engineering, a situation in which one or more quality attributes apply to more than one product dimension. It can apply to actions and data in multiple candidate solutions—for example, audit, authentication, security, and localization. Also referred to as a cross-cutting concern.

customer partner: *see* partner.

customer validation: *see* validated learning.

cycle time: in software development, a concept from Lean manufacturing that measures the delay between the start of work and delivery to the customer. *See also* lead time.

D

data attribute: an aspect of data that is specific to a data entity needed to support business activities.

data dictionary: defines data attributes needed by a product.

Data Dimension: *see* Data Product Dimension.

data domain: any important topic that a product acts on and needs to save.

data entity: a group of related pieces of information to be stored by the system.

data example: provides concrete, specific data used to explore, evaluate, and confirm product needs.

data model: shows the logical structures of data—domains (or entities) and relationships—independently of the data design. It is also known as a *fact model.*

Data Product Dimension: the product dimension that represents the product's repository of data and useful information.

data relationship: a business rule that links two data domains or entities.

decision table: specifies a set of conditions to reach a business conclusion.

decision tree: illustrates a set of conditions to reach a business conclusion.

delivery: work that transforms one or more allocated candidate solutions into a releasable portion or version of the product.

delivery cycle: time period for completing and releasing one or more candidate solutions.

delivery horizon: time period for a delivery cycle, such as a release or iteration, in which portions, or increments, of the product are completed. *See also* delivery cycle.

delivery method: a technique or theory for sequencing the delivery of a product.

delivery team: the technology partners who design, build, buy, test, deploy, deliver, and support the product.

dependency: a relationship between two elements in which one is reliant on the other.

dependency graph: visualizes relationships between elements in which one element (the client) requires or depends on another element (the supplier).

development environment: a subset of the Environment Dimension that represents the technology platforms (hardware, software, and standards) that govern how a product will be architected, developed, tested, deployed, and released into service.

development quality attribute: a subset of the quality attribute dimension that represents properties needed to develop the product.

discovery: work that explores, evaluates, and confirms product options for potential delivery. Also referred to as *product discovery.*

domain: the area of interest that a product addresses.

done: *see* acceptance criteria.

doneness criteria: *see* acceptance criteria.

E

efficiency: a quality attribute that defines how well the product utilizes processor capacity, disk space, memory, bandwidth, and other resources.

ends: the desired outcomes expressed in the product's vision, goals, and objectives. Ends describe and quantify a product's anticipated value.

Environment Dimension: *see* Environment Product Dimension.

Environment Product Dimension: the product dimension that represents how a product conforms to physical properties and technology platforms.

event: a trigger that causes the business to respond.

example: a scenario that contains actual data values.

external risk: *see* risk.

external roadmap: a subset of the internal product roadmap that is used to engage or acquire customers, investors, and external partners, to promote market innovation, or to shake up the market.

F

facilitated workshop: a structured meeting in which product partners collaborate to plan and analyze product needs with the guidance of a skilled, neutral facilitator.

fact model: *see* data model.

feature: a cohesive bundle of externally visible functionality that aligns with business goals and objectives (Gottesdiener, 2005).

flexibility: a quality attribute that defines the ability of the product to be augmented, extended, and expanded with functionality or users.

flow: in Lean and Kanban, the uninterrupted forward motion of work facilitated by pull, whereby downstream activities control workflow through work-in-progress limits.

flow delivery: product method using flow. *See also* flow.

functional product dimension: an aspect of a product that expresses product capabilities, or things that the product must do for its users. Includes the Users, Actions, Data, and Controls Product Dimensions.

G

given-when-then (GWT): expresses a scenario with data, including the pre- and postconditions.

glossary: a collection of business terms and concepts relevant to a product, along with their definitions.

glossary guardian: someone responsible for ensuring the accuracy and completeness of the glossary's terms and definitions.

goal: a desired high-level product outcome or target result that is quantified by objectives.

H

high-assurance product: a product that is governed by regulatory oversight, involves critical safety and security needs, or must prevent software or hardware anomalies that might allow a catastrophic event.

hypothesis: a supposition concerning the value of a candidate solution.

I

increment: a portion or partial implementation of a product.

inheritance hierarchy: shows the types (supertypes and subtypes) of a data entity.

input queue: *see* product backlog.

installability: a quality attribute that defines the ability and ease with which software and hardware can be loaded into a target environment.

interaction matrix: a means to explore, evaluate, and confirm the expected effects of actions on data.

Interface Dimension: *see* Interface Product Dimension.

Interface Product Dimension: the product dimension that represents a product's means of connection with users, systems, and devices.

internal risk: *see* risk.

internal roadmap: a product plan that is used to communicate with internal stakeholders.

iteration: a single development cycle, usually one to four weeks, resulting in a deployable candidate solution. Each iteration (or sprint in Scrum vernacular) encapsulates a cycle of product discovery and delivery for one or more candidate solutions.

iteration plan: the plan for work to be completed during an iteration. Also called *sprint plan.*

interoperability: a quality attribute that defines the ease with which a product can exchange data or services with other systems (including communication protocols, hardware, other software applications, and data compatibility layers).

J

journey: a scenario that describes the overall sequence of a user's experience with a product.

K

Kanban: an Agile software engineering approach in which a visual management system is used to promote evolutionary changes in software development, to reduce risk, and to enable faster delivery by pulling work through stages based on capacity (Anderson, 2010).

Kanban Method: *see* Kanban.

Kanban System: *see* Kanban.

L

lead time: in software development, a concept borrowed from Lean manufacturing that measures the delay between request and delivery to the customer. *See also* cycle time.

Lean: in software development, a technique that focuses on delivering value, eliminating waste, reducing delays, improving product quality, and enabling continual process improvement.

Lean startup: a trademarked term for a method using Lean thinking and Agile development practices for entrepreneurial products in order to lower development costs and increases business value by frequently delivering and validating small increments of the product (Reis, 2011).

logical data model: a comprehensive rendering of a product's detailed data requirements needed to support behavior, control, and interface requirements. *See also* data model.

M

market segment: a portion of a market that shares characteristics relevant to your product.

means: the ways to deliver the desired outcomes (ends).

mental model: a conceptual representation of how something works in the real world.

minimum marketable feature (MMF): the smallest set of functionality that is valued by customers and returns value when independently released (Denne and Cleland-Huang, 2003).

minimum viable product (MVP): one or more minimum marketable features released as a product.

MMF: *see* minimum marketable feature.

modifiability: a quality attribute that defines the ability to correct defects, repair, add new functionality, or perform product support functions; the ability to modify the product without taking it out of service.

motif: *see* theme.

MVP: *see* minimum viable product.

N

nonfunctional product dimensions: aspects of a product that express properties that the product must have; the Interface, Environment, and Quality Attribute Dimensions.

Now-View: the planning horizon with the shortest delivery cycle.

O

objective: a specific measure that quantifies the goals of a product.

one piece flow: a Lean concept in which a team minimizes waste by completing one work item before beginning work on another.

operational environment: a subset of the Environment Dimension that represents the in-use product's physical properties and technology platforms.

operational prototype: a partial or preliminary version of a product deployed to the operational environments.

operational Quality Attribute: a subset of the Quality Attribute Dimension that represents properties needed to operate a product.

option: *see* product option.

option, product: *see* product option.

Options board: a visual space, usually mounted on a wall, used by a team to explore and evaluate product options. The 7 Product Dimensions icons are placed along the top; below is space for writing and drawing representations of the 7 Product Dimensions.

P

partner: someone who collaborates to discover and deliver a product; may come from the business, the technical, or the customer realm.

partner, business: a partner who authorizes, legitimates, or pays for product development or for the purchase of a commercial software product; typically, a business or product manager.

partner, customer: a partner who uses a product, buys the product, or advises on the purchase of the product.

partner, technology: a partner who designs, builds, buys, tests, deploys, delivers, or supports a product.

partnership: the collaborative group of product partners.

performance: a quality attribute that defines how well a product executes. Can be decomposed into speed of response, throughput, storage capacity, and execution time.

persona: a written description of a typical user's background, including relevant details such as needs and goals.

Planguage: a keyword-driven language designed to specify product needs quantitatively in natural language.

plan: the partner's best estimate of what might be delivered during a given planning horizon to achieve value.

planning horizon: the period of time a plan covers; may be strategic (for the entire product), mid-range (for a release) or tactical (for immediate delivery).

planning view: a planning perspective for delivering product options.

portability: a quality attribute that defines the ease of moving a product to other machines, operating systems, language versions, compilers, and so on.

portfolio roadmap: an evolving plan of the products to be developed as part of an organization's product portfolio.

postcondition: the defined state of data or a system after an action has ended.

precondition: the defined state of data or a system that must be true before an action can begin.

Pre-View: the planning horizon focused on a medium-range delivery cycle.

product: a software application, system, or device containing software that provides value to customers and business partners.

product backlog: a catalog or queue containing unrealized product options at varying levels of detail.

product capabilities: *see* capability.

product champion: a product partner who balances all the perspectives, reconciles any differences, and makes final decisions about the product.

product dimension: *see* 7 Product Dimensions.

product discovery: *see* discovery.

product need: something a product partner thinks will satisfy a goal or objective.

product option: a potential product need.

product owner: *see* product champion.

product partner: *see* partner.

product partnership: *see* partnership.

product queue: *see* product backlog.

product roadmap: an evolving plan of product releases, with brief descriptions of their themes and features. The roadmap is intended to realize the product vision over time and satisfy goals and objectives.

product team: the group of business, customer, and business partners who collaborate to discover and deliver a product.

product vision: *see* vision.

product: a software application or system, or device containing software that provides value to users who interact with it.

prototype: a representation of a product.

pull: in Kanban, the act of withdrawing work from an upstream queue only when the downstream activity has the capacity to work on it, based on work-in-progress limits.

Q

Quality Attribute Dimension: *see* Quality Attribute Product Dimension.

Quality Attribute Product Dimension: the product dimension that represents certain properties that qualify a product's operation and development.

quality attribute scenario: characterizes quality attributes as high-level scenarios using a templated specification.

queue: holding area or buffer. In Kanban, a queue is a holding area waiting for a downstream activity. *See also* product backlog.

R

recoverability: a quality attribute that defines a product's ability to recover from failures such as checkpoints, restarts, and backups.

regulation: a law, rule, or order prescribed by a government or organizational authority.

relationship map: shows the relationships among an organization's functions and with external entities (customers and providers).

release: a version of a product deployed for use.

reliability: a quality attribute that defines the probability that a product will execute without failure.

requirement: a product option that has been selected for the current delivery cycle.

response: a predefined action that an event triggers.

retrospective: a process improvement practice used by teams to reflect on a process or product and improve it.

reusability: a quality attribute that defines the ability to use or convert product components in other systems.

risk: a potential adverse occurrence or condition that endangers the success of a product. External risks are related to customers, markets, and regulations; internal risks are related to the people and technologies involved in delivering the product.

roadmap: *see* product roadmap.

robustness: a quality attribute that defines the degree to which a product continues to function properly when confronted by failures such as unexpected operation conditions, invalid inputs, or interrupts in hardware or software components.

S

safety: a quality attribute that defines a product's ability to protect users and the environment from harm.

scalability: a quality attribute that defines the ability to expand the number of users or increase a product's capabilities without making significant changes to the application software.

scenario: a text description of an instance of use.

scenario Z pattern: uses scenarios as a path to explore options across planning views.

security: a quality attribute that defines a product's ability to resist unauthorized, accidental, or unintended usage while providing access to legitimate users.

sprint: *see* iteration.

sprint plan: *see* iteration plan.

sponsor: a business partner who authorizes, legitimates, or pays for product development or the purchase of a commercial software product.

state: a defined condition of a data entity or user role.

state diagram: shows the allowable transitions from one data state to another.

stakeholder: anyone with a stake or interest in a product. *See also* partner.

story: a product need expressed as a user's goal.

story map: organizes stories in logical order using two dimensions: usage sequence and business importance.

strategy: a long-term plan or course of action intended to fulfill an organization's goals and objectives.

structured conversation: a framework that guides product partners as they learn about a product's possibilities and decide what to deliver. Also called discovery, pruning, preparing, optioning, or refining product options.

subtype: an aspect of data that details its unique attributes and relationships and inherits its supertype's attributes and relationships.

supertype: an aspect of data that encapsulates data and relationships that are common to all types in that class.

T

technical debt: the cost incurred to enhance or maintain software that was initially delivered quickly.

technology partner: *see* partner.

technology platform: the set of software, hardware, and standards that comprise a product's development and operational environments.

testability: a quality attribute that defines the ease of testing product components or an entire product for defects.

theme: a unifying expression used to describe and organize a delivery cycle.

timebox delivery: product delivery using a fixed period of time.

U

upstream: in Kanban, the originating or predecessor location from which work has evolved.

usability: a quality attribute that defines the ease with which users use a product effectively.

use case: describes how a user's goal is achieved through interacting with the product.

user: a person, another product, or a system that interacts with a product.

user acceptance test: *see* acceptance test.

User Dimension: *see* User Product Dimension.

user experience: an overarching term for understanding a user's product interactions and context of use.

User Product Dimension: the product dimension that represents the users who interact with the product.

user role: represents a specific way a user interacts with a product.

user role map: visually represents the types of user roles and the relationships among them.

user story: *see* story.

V

validate: *see* validation.

validated learning: checking the delivered solution's actual results against its anticipated value and adjusting delivery plans based on the findings.

validation: in product development, to use evidence to confirm that the delivered product satisfies its intended use and delivers its intended value; validation ensures that you have built the right product.

validation, customer: *see* validated learning.

value: fair return in exchange for time, money, goods, or services.

value consideration: a variable used to assess the value of a product option.

value decision: a determination about product options as a result of synthesizing value considerations, benefits, and risks.

value stream: all of the activities conducted to discover and deliver an organization's products and services to customers.

value stream map: shows the end-to-end sequence and movement of information, materials, and actions in the value stream.

value tool: a qualitative or quantitative technique useful for making value decisions about product options.

velocity: the rate at which product development work is completed within a delivery cycle.

verify: in product development, using acceptance criteria to confirm that the product is build according to its expected outcomes; verification ensures that you have built the software correctly.

vision: articulates the long-term concept of a product.

W

WIP: *see* work-in-progress.

work-in-progress (WIP): unfinished work item or an item waiting in a queue to be worked on.

work-in-progress (WIP) limits: in software development, a threshold that limits the number of unfinished items that can be worked on at one time.

workflow board: a visual space, usually mounted on a wall, used by the team to show the state of product backlog items as they are being discovered and delivered. *See also* Kanban.

workshop: *see* facilitated workshop.

REFERENCES

Anderson, David J. 2010. *Kanban: Successful Evolutionary Change for Your Technology Business*. Seattle: Blue Hole Press.

Appelo, Jurgen. 2012. *Management 3.0: Leading Agile Developers, Developing Agile Leaders*. New York: Addison-Wesley.

Barbacci, Mario R., Robert Ellison, Anthony J. Lattanze, Judith A. Stafford, Charles B. Weinstock, and William G. Wood. 2003. *Quality Attribute Workshops (QAWs)*, third edition, Software Engineering Institute, Technical Report CMU SEI-2003-TR-016 ESC-TR-2003-016, August. [Available at http://www.sei.cmu.edu/]

Bass, Len, Paul Clements, and Rick Kazman. 2003. *Software Architecture in Practice*, second edition. New York: Addison-Wesley.

Beyer, Hugh, and Karen Holtzblatt. 1997. *Contextual Design: Defining Customer-Centered Systems*. Burlington, MA: Morgan Kaufmann.

Blank, Gary Steven. 2007. *The Four Steps to the Epiphany: Successful Strategies for Products that Win*, third edition. Café Press.

Denne, Mark, and Jane Cleland-Huang. 2003. *Software by Numbers: Low-Risk, High-Return Development*. Upper Saddle River, NJ: Prentice Hall.

Gane, Chris, and Trish Sarson. 1979. *Structured Systems Analysis: Tools and Techniques*. Upper Saddle River, NJ: Prentice Hall.

Gilb, Thomas. 2005. *Competitive Engineering: A Handbook for Systems Engineering, Requirements Engineering, and Software Engineering Using Planguage*. Oxford, UK: Butterworth-Heinemann.

Gottesdiener, Ellen. 2002. *Requirements by Collaboration: Workshops for Defining Needs*. New York: Addison-Wesley.

Gottesdiener, Ellen. 2005. *The Software Requirements Memory Jogger: A Pocket Guide to Help Software and Business Teams Develop and Manage Requirements*. Salem, NH: GOAL/QPC.

Moore, Geoffrey A. 2006. *Crossing the Chasm: Marketing and Selling Disruptive Products to Mainstream Customers*. New York: HarperBusiness.

Osterwalder, Alexander, and Yves Pigneur. 2010. *Business Model Generation: A Handbook for Visionaries, Game Changers, and Challengers*. New York: Wiley.

Pixton, Pollyanna, Niel Nickolaisen, Todd Little, and Kent McDonald. 2009. *Stand Back and Deliver: Accelerating Business Agility*. New York: Addison-Wesley.

Poppendieck, Mary, and Tom Poppendieck. 2009. *Leading Lean Software Development: Results Are Not the Point*. New York: Addison-Wesley.

Reinertsen, Donald G. 2009. *The Principles of Product Development Flow: Second Generation Lean Product Development*. Redondo Beach, CA: Celeritas Publishing.

Reis, Eric. 2011. *The Lean Startup: How Today's Entrepreneurs Use Continuous Innovation to Create Radically Successful Businesses*. London: Crown Business.

Rüping, Andreas. 2003. *Agile Documentation: A Pattern Guide to Producing Lightweight Documents for Software Projects*. New York: John Wiley & Sons.

INDEX

NUMBERS AND SYMBOLS

A

B

E

F

G

H

I

J

Q

R

S

T

U